American Country Christmas

COMPILED & EDITED BY
BRENDA WALDRON KOLB

Oxmoor House®

©1993 by Oxmoor House, Inc.
Book Division of Southern Progress Corporation
P.O. Box 2463, Birmingham, Alabama 35201

Published by Oxmoor House, Inc., and Leisure Arts, Inc.

Library of Congress Catalog Number: 89-61909
Hardcover ISBN: 0-8487-1111-4
Softcover ISBN: 0-8487-1186-6
ISSN: 1044-4904
Manufactured in the United States of America
Second Printing

Editor-in-Chief: Nancy J. Fitzpatrick
Senior Homes Editor: Mary Kay Culpepper
Senior Editor, Editorial Services: Olivia Kindig Wells
Director of Manufacturing: Jerry Higdon
Art Director: James Boone

American Country Christmas

Editor: Brenda Waldron Kolb
Assistant Editor: Lelia Gray Neil
Editorial Assistant: Janica Lynn York
Copy Chief: Mary Jean Haddin
Copy Editor: Susan Smith Cheatham
Copy Assistant: Leslee Rester Johnson
Designer: Elizabeth Passey Edge
Senior Photographer: John O'Hagan
Photostylist: Katie Stoddard
Production Manager: Rick Litton
Associate Production Manager: Theresa L. Beste
Production Assistant: Marianne Jordan
Recipe Development: Debby Maugans, Elizabeth Taliaferro
Test Kitchen Home Economist: Elizabeth T. Luckett
Recipe Editor: Caroline A. Grant
Artists: Barbara Ball, Eleanor Cameron, Carol O. Loria,
    Michael W. Thomas, Karen Tindall Tillery

*Cover: For information on ordering beeswax tapers, candle
clips, or greenery, see the source listings on page 152.*

Contents

$\mathcal{A}$s every child knows, Santa Claus and his elves work very hard. And as one of Santa's helpers, you also work hard to create a special season for your family and friends. ◆ That's why we've filled this new edition of *American Country Christmas* with terrific projects, recipes, and gift foods, and we've added practical information on how to make this Christmas the best ever. ◆ For presents you'll be proud to give to anyone on your list, stitch, crochet, or glue ornaments like those on Grandmother's tree. Whip up zesty salsas and spreads, or bake a batch of what may be the world's best cookies. ◆ As Christmas draws nearer, deck your halls with dried-fruit topiaries and gorgeous wreaths made from dried flowers and grasses. We've introduced step-by-step photographs and greatly expanded the source listings to make it easy for you. ◆ So welcome to this year's *American Country Christmas.* Here you'll find everything you need to create holiday magic you and your loved ones will long remember.

Brenda W. Kolb

*Instructions for
making a dried wreath
are on pages 6–7.*

Country Christmas at Home

WREATH-MAKING WORKSHOP

◆

A WINTER REVELATION

◆

SEASON'S GREENINGS

◆

CANDLES DRESSED
IN SILVER AND GOLD

◆

IDEAS: OUTDOOR DECOR, NATURALLY

A Natural Joy In Texas

Joy Jowell transforms an everyday harvest into stunning wreaths and floral decorations.

Weeds—the common term for the grasses that grow wild on the Texas plains—are the backbone of Joy's business. She owns the Texas General Store in Seabrook, located between Houston and Galveston.

Step into her shop at Christmastime, and you are instantly met with the exhilarating fragrances of cinnamon, citrus, and cedar. The scents come from huge bins of potpourri located in the heart of the store. The names alone make you feel good—Sweet Apple Annie, Piney Woods, Orange Marmalade, and Christmas at Home.

The store is where Joy works her magic. She combines her simple weeds and grasses, which have been gathered from the plains and beside railroad tracks, with lush materials such as dried pomegranates, oranges, apples, and hot peppers to make distinctive decorations for the home.

Stay even a little while, and you'll catch the inventive energy shared by Joy and her employees. "Everyone has a creative edge," she says. "We are fortunate to be able to use this creativity daily in what we make."

Joy's love of the earth and what it yields began when she was growing up in Lamesa, Texas. The land was so flat that as a child she believed she could see to the ends of the earth. Joy thinks that it was the lack of rich foliage that led her to make do with the materials she had, thus turning tumbleweeds into decorative treasures.

Above: This jolly grouping of Santas greets guests as they enter Joy's living room. The bold red cupboard was made by Seabrook artist and gatherer Butch Robins (see source listing on page 152). A single candle encircled by a tallowberry wreath illuminates this display.

Left: A market basket of native grasses displays the rich foliage that grows along the highways and interstates in the Houston area. From left to right, timothy grass, white rice grass, blue salvia, red cockscomb, bladder beans, chinaberries, Texas red peppers, and broom weed make up Joy's vignette.

"We have a deep reverence for the earth and its gifts—we never strip the land bare," assures Joy. When gathering, Joy and her crew follow a rule of threes: "We take one for ourselves, leave one for the birds, and leave one for the Master Gardener."

This creed is strictly followed by her gatherers, a diverse group of people from all over the state who reap weeds in their spare time. The group includes the president of a bank who harvests clover, a schoolteacher who picks chinaberries from her backyard tree, and a sea captain who finds curly dock and sea lavender.

Since its official opening in 1981, her business has blossomed, expanding from trade show and retail into mail order and wholesale markets. In fact, the past Christmas season was her most successful ever.

The secret of her business success is simple. "I want my customers to have the very best," Joy proudly says. "We feel that what we create is a part of who we are. We strive to make things that are better than what you could find anywhere else."

Her home, located only a few minutes from her shop, is as delightful as Joy herself. She uses her natural decorations to enhance it—swags drape the entry to the living room as well as the mantel, and every room is graced with a wreath. Her Christmas tree is decorated simply with red canella, white tallow berries, and sheer white ribbon.

Joy does not hesitate to share the secrets of her designs. First, she believes that "beauty is in the eye of the beholder." That's why she enjoys using materials that others would have thrown away. Second, she obeys a "natural" law. "The piece should have an effortless flow to it," she says. "The shape of the branches or flowers should determine the shape of the design."

Color and texture are also important to her work. Joy blends splashes of vibrant color, such as paprika berry, with earth-tone grasses. Finally, she always considers where the piece will be placed. Dried arrangements will last indefinitely but should not receive direct sunlight. They will fade with time, but Joy thinks this only adds to their beauty—"like character wrinkles," she says.

Take into account these hints as you use nature's bounties to create your own dried masterpieces. On the following pages Joy demonstrates the making of one of her best-selling wreaths.

Below: Garlands from the Texas General Store, Joy's shop, festoon the mantel. Her house is a collection of things she loves, most handmade by friends. The Jonah and the Whale on the table was hand-carved for her by fellow Texan P. J. Hornberger (see source listing on page 152).

Wreath-Making Workshop

Follow these step-by-step photographs as Joy Jowell demonstrates the easy process of crafting a natural wreath. To order the materials used here—or, if you're short on time, to get a finished wreath—see the source listing on page 152.

To prepare for making your wreath, assemble the following tools and materials: a plain vine wreath, assorted dried materials, florist's wire, wire clippers, greenery clippers, and a hot-glue gun (if desired).

Step 1: Position a small bundle of grasses on a plain vine wreath. Wrap florist's wire tightly around the wreath several times to secure.

Do not cut the wire; add the next bundle and continue wrapping with florist's wire.

Joy uses neutral-colored grasses such as broom weed, lil rush, and hornbeck to build a thick base.

Step 2: Continue wiring bundles to the wreath, positioning bundles with the stems fanning toward the inside and outside of the wreath.

With greenery clippers, trim excess ends of stems before wiring on the next bundle. Joy is shown cutting the long stems of a chinaberry bundle.

Step 3: As you fill out the wreath, check to see that colors and types of grasses/flowers are evenly placed around the wreath. Make sure, too, that the thickness of the wreath is consistent.

For a colorful accent, tuck in stems of blue salvia and crimson cockscomb, hot-gluing them if desired.

Step 4: After the wreath is complete, clip the wire and tuck it into the back of the wreath.

Other materials used on this wreath are shore rush, timothy grass, bladder bean pods, and tallow berry.

Note how the cockscomb, blue salvia, and tallow berry provide dynamic contrast against the earth-tone grasses of this splendid natural wreath.

A Winter Revelation

At last! The snow has cleared, and these lyrical creatures are reveling in the first blooms of the season. This pillow will delight you, too, from winter into spring— thanks to its charming combination of color and fabric.

Materials:
patterns on pages 128–29
½ **yard (60"-wide) blue-gray tweed wool for pillow front**
½ **yard (60"-wide) green plaid wool for pillow back**
⅓ **yard (60"-wide) green wool or wool felt for ground**
scraps of wool or wool felt: red, yellow, cream, purple, lavender
red thread
9 black seed beads
⅛ **yard (60"-wide) red wool or wool felt for flange**
polyester stuffing

Note: Finished size of pillow is 16" square. All seam allowances are ½". To prevent cut edges from raveling, before using wool pieces, machine-wash them in hot water. Rinse in cold water and then machine-dry.

From blue-gray wool, cut a 15" square for pillow front. From green plaid wool, cut a 15" square for pillow back.

Enlarge and transfer ground pattern to green wool and cut out. Transfer appliqué patterns to wool scraps as indicated and cut out.

Aligning raw edges, pin ground piece to pillow front. Referring to pattern, position appliqué pieces on pillow front, tucking ends of flower stems, bird's legs, and bottom edge of chipmunk under top edge of ground piece. Pin in place to secure. Using red thread, blanket-stitch pieces to pillow front.

Referring to pattern, stitch 1 seed bead each to chipmunk and bird for eyes, and remaining beads to flower center.

For zigzag flange, from red wool, cut 4 (3" x 15") strips. Along 1 edge of 1 strip, mark and cut a zigzag edge with 6 points (see photograph). Repeat for remaining strips.

With right sides facing, raw edges aligned, and points toward center, stitch 1 zigzag strip to 1 edge of pillow front. Repeat for remaining strips.

To finish pillow, with right sides facing, raw edges aligned, and flange toward center, stitch pillow front to pillow back, leaving an opening for turning. Trim corners, and turn. Stuff moderately. Slipstitch opening closed.

Season's Greenings

An inventive yet practical woman, Noreen Wint of Lancaster, Pennsylvania, relies on the bounty of nature for her Christmas decorations. Here she shares the how-tos behind her creations.

Most everyone knows someone like Noreen. Creative and energetic, she's a gifted gardener, an inspired cook, and a consummate collector. Her flair extends to decorating, a talent that shines especially at Christmas, when her home glows with the sights and scents of the season.

And she makes it all look easy.

In Noreen's case, what looks easy really is. That's because when it comes to decking the halls, she believes in using what she finds in her own pantry, toolbox, and backyard.

There is one exception to Noreen's keep-it-simple philosophy: the family's 14-foot Christmas tree. "It's quite something," admits Noreen with a laugh, "but we do love it. After Frank, my husband, inherited his share of his mother's wonderful ornament collection, we just kept adding to it." More than 1,500 ornaments later, the Wints' current tree is simply dazzling.

Noreen's other holiday customs are much simpler, and she takes care to blend her husband's family traditions with her own. Says Noreen, "When I was growing up in Ireland during World War II, holly and ivy were the only materials we had for decorating, and I still like to use them as a remembrance of those times."

And as her decorations show, Noreen continues to employ nature's gifts with creativity and style. Turn the page to learn how she does it.

Right: "It's probably best to let the sugared fruit dry on a rack for several hours or even overnight before placing it in the arrangement," grants Noreen, "but I'm too impatient for that. As long as I'm careful not to move the fruit around too much, it looks fine."

Left: Noreen's fondness for classic designs is seen in her live ivy topiaries and simple wreath, which contrast effectively with the family's extravagantly decorated tree.

Festive Fruit

Noreen's tabletop arrangement of sugared fruit is a perfect example of her penchant for using what she has on hand. To construct the base, she simply stacks several pedestaled cake stands of different sizes, with the largest on bottom and the smallest on top. (Adhesive putty stabilizes them.) After rolling each piece of fruit in lightly beaten egg whites and then in granulated sugar, Noreen places it on the base. For contrast, she also adds a few unsugared pomegranates and a pineapple.

Noreen builds this tower of sugared fruit in minutes, but it lasts for a couple of weeks (the sugar coating seems to preserve the fruit). After that, the materials can be washed and then recycled into a fruit salad.

A Winning Wreath

The simple holly-and-ivy wreath that hangs over Noreen's fireplace couldn't be easier to make. First, she constructs a large foundation of several loops of heavy-gauge wire, taping the ends of the wire together to secure them. So that her wreath will be in proportion with the great tree and lofty ceilings, Noreen sizes the foundation generously.

After cutting long lengths of ivy and sprigs of holly from her garden, Noreen wraps long tendrils of ivy around the foundation, using short lengths of florist's wire to hold them in place. Then she simply tucks in the holly all around the wreath. That's all there is to it.

Although the wreath's ivy base holds up for months, says Noreen, the holly needs to be replaced once a week or so.

A Midwinter's Garden

A bit more involved—but still quite workable—is Noreen's miniature winter garden. She begins with a birdbath sans pedestal. (A large, shallow dish also works well.) About six weeks before Christmas, Noreen fills it with potting soil and plants grass seed leftover from the summer before.

Once the grass sprouts, she "plants" branches of corkscrew willow, pansies, and cuttings of paperwhites placed in florist's water-pick tubes. Moss and ivy encircle the whole. "The willow, moss, and ivy I cut from the yard," explains Noreen, "and every winter I grow pansies and start trays of paperwhites in my cold frame." Even the material for the tiny bird's nest aloft in the branches is close at hand—Noreen fashions it from a bundle of birdweed.

As Christmas draws near, Noreen usually strings tiny white lights along the twisting willow branches of her miniature winter garden. She keeps the soil barely damp (not soggy), and the garden stays beautiful for at least two months.

Together these natural decorations make for a home that is definitely decked out for Christmas—and all without midnight crafting sessions and frazzled nerves. "I like to keep it simple," says Noreen. "After all, decorating for the holidays is supposed to be fun!"

Chilly Cheer from a Canvas Snowman

He prepares to brave the cold with his woolen scarf and floppy hat, but this steadfast snowman stays inside. Snuggle him into a cozy chair, or stand him proudly in a window.

Materials:
patterns on pages 130–31
tracing paper
water-soluble marker
½ yard (45"-wide) white lightweight canvas or heavy sheeting
8½" x 11" piece of black felt
thread to match fabrics
sawdust or sand
waxed paper
newspaper
acrylic paints: antique white, burnt umber, black, brick red
paintbrushes: medium and small
craft glue
1 (1½" x 21") piece of red wool

Note: Finished size of snowman is 14" tall. Patterns include ¼" seam allowances.

Using tracing paper, transfer patterns and markings to fabrics and cut out.

With right sides facing, raw edges aligned, and using 12 or more stitches per inch, machine-stitch body front to body back, leaving bottom open as indicated. Clip curves and turn. Holding snowman upside down, stuff firmly with sawdust to within 4" of bottom edge. Pin bottom edge closed. Turn snowman right side up to determine if body is stuffed firmly enough. (Body is firm enough when head does not flop; add more sawdust if necessary.) To make a flat base, fold in sides and bottom edges of snowman as if wrapping a package: Referring to Diagram 1, fold in sides of body. Referring to Diagram 2, overlap front body edge over back body edge. Turn raw edge under ½" and whipstitch bottom seams closed.

To paint snowman, first dust off any loose particles of sawdust from snowman's body. Lay waxed paper over newspaper to prevent body from sticking to work surface. Paint entire body antique white. Apply several coats, letting dry between applications.

To achieve antique effect, mix 1 part water and 1 part burnt umber (mixture should be thin and watery). Apply lightly and quickly to entire surface of snowman. Lay snowman on an old towel and, working quickly with rags, blot excess paint. Repeat process until you are satisfied with antique look. Let dry.

Referring to photograph and using a small paintbrush, paint eyes, mouth, and buttons black. Paint nose brick red. Let dry.

For hat, with raw edges aligned, stitch crown pieces together, leaving long edge open as indicated. Clip curves and corners and turn. Slip crown through opening in hat brim. With raw edges aligned and easing curve along edge, stitch crown to brim. To secure seam allowance, finger-press seam allowance upward. Topstitch on *outside* of hat, ⅛" above brim seam. Glue hat to snowman's head.

To make scarf fringe, make ½"-long clips into ends of wool fabric, spacing clips ⅛" apart. Fray ends. Tie scarf around snowman's neck.

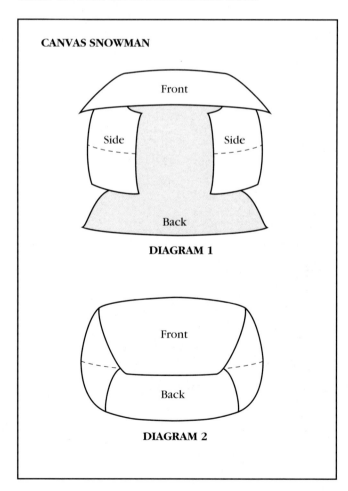

CANVAS SNOWMAN

Front

Side   Side

Back

DIAGRAM 1

Front

Back

DIAGRAM 2

Wright at Home for Christmas

It's always a pleasure to see the Frank Lloyd Wright Home and Studio in Oak Park, Illinois—the birthplace of American residential architecture. But Christmas visitors find much more than innovative designs. They discover a family's love for Christmas.

In 1889, young Frank Lloyd Wright built a modest cottage for his 18-year-old bride, Catherine Tobin. Over the years, his home expanded as his family grew, and holiday celebrations with his six children became as exciting as Wright's architectural designs. Today, yuletide tours of his Oak Park home give visitors a glimpse of the Wright family's Christmas traditions. (For the address and phone number of this and other Frank Lloyd Wright sites, see the box on page 18; for a gift catalog, see page 152.)

Like many of their contemporaries, the Wrights decorated their home with cedar swags, holly wreaths, and arrangements of dried weeds and grasses. Today, horticultural students re-create these arrangements, and interpreters from a local school lead the Christmas tours of the house. A tradition for many area families, the tours reveal a surprising contrast between the austere architecture for which Wright later became known and his exuberant Christmas celebrations.

Wright holidays required a great deal of preparation by the entire family. One of Catherine's Christmas projects was forcing paperwhites. (For more information on forcing paperwhites and other bulbs, see pages 126–27.) She also made gifts of pincushions, needle cases, and sachets from fabric samples. Catherine encouraged her children to make presents for family members, and they joined her in crafting pomanders and beaded necklaces. And, since the children loved to make sweets, the cook relinquished the domain of her kitchen so they could make fudge, divinity, and pulled taffy. While Catherine kept the children busy with these projects, Wright secretly wrapped presents for them.

The biggest family project was decorating the 10-foot tree in the barrel-vaulted playroom. A gymnasium, concert hall, theater, and home school all in one, the playroom was the center of family activities, especially during the holidays. On Christmas Eve, the children hung their stockings under an

Left: Shown here are Frank Lloyd Wright, his wife, Catherine, and members of the Wright family.

Right: Wright is usually remembered for defying convention, and he did so even by replacing the usual small tabletop tree with a large, freestanding one. The vaulted playroom ceiling allowed the Wrights to decorate a tall tree with candy canes, glass balls, and icicles.

Arabian Night–inspired mural. In the early dawn of Christmas morning, Wright lit the candles that decorated the tree, turning it into a fairyland of glimmering lights. The eager children stood beneath the mistletoe in the doorway and envisioned the new toys that would later fill the built-in toy chests under the bay windows. They rushed to empty their stockings filled with oranges, apples, nuts, spiced cakes, and cookies. Wright laughed as the children then

unwrapped small gifts he had cleverly disguised in huge packages.

Once the presents were opened, the family would enjoy a traditional turkey dinner in the dining room. Afterward, the Wrights would return to the playroom and dance around the tree, singing carols.

Many of Wright's playful holiday traditions continue to be celebrated today. Volunteers at Oak Park serenade their neighbors during the season, and children make decorations and refreshments similar to those the Wright children made a century ago. The home's structure represents the beginning of an architectural style that literally changed the face of America, but it was also a place where the faces of children brightened with the magic of Christmas.

Above: The Wright family ate Christmas dinner in the first interior in which Wright designed every element. Each child's place setting included a traditional Christmas cracker (for more about such crackers, see pages 116–17).

Wright Sites

Known as the father of modern architecture, Frank Lloyd Wright designed numerous structures across the country in his revolutionary style. Many of these buildings are open and decorated for the holidays. Contact the sites listed below for further information:

Frank Lloyd Wright Home
  and Studio
951 Chicago Avenue
Oak Park, IL 60302
(708) 848-1500

Unity Temple
875 Lake Street
Oak Park, IL 60301
(708) 848-6225

Taliesin West
108th Street and Cactus Road
Scottsdale, AZ 85261
(602) 860-2700

First Christian Church
6750 N. Seventh Avenue
Phoenix, AZ 85013
(602) 246-9206

Community Christian
  Church
4601 Main Street
Kansas City, MO 64112
(816) 561-6531

Samuel Freeman House
1962 Glencoe Way
Los Angeles, CA 90068
(213) 851-0671

Allen-Lambe House Museum
  and Study Center
255 N. Roosevelt
Wichita, KS 67208
(316) 687-1027

Florida Southern College
  Planetarium
111 Lake Hollingsworth Drive
Lakeland, FL 33801-5698
(813) 680-4118

Stanley and Mildred
  Rosenbaum House
601 Riverview Drive
Florence, AL 35630
(205) 764-5274

A Garland to Pine For

Bring the outdoors inside this season by creating a rustic decoration with natural materials. This swag of stars is fashioned from dried pine needles, twine, and bright red beads.

Materials:
long-needle pine straw
red pearl cotton
lightweight twine
large-eyed crewel needle
11 (½") red wooden beads

For 1 star, divide pine straw into 5 bundles with 9 single needles in each bundle. Using pearl cotton, wrap and tie ends of each bundle together.

Referring to photograph, place pine-straw bundles in a star formation.

Using pearl cotton, wrap and tie ends of bundles together. Trim ends of needles even. Repeat to make 8 stars.

For garland, cut twine desired length, adding extra for securing end beads and for hanging.

Thread needle with twine. Leaving a long tail, string 1 bead onto twine, loop twine around bead, and run needle back through bead to secure.

String 1 more bead in the same manner, and then string 1 star by pushing needle through tied ends of 2 pine straw points.

Continue alternating stars and beads. Finish garland by securing end bead.

Candles Dressed in Silver and Gold

Shimmering ribbon and natural accents surround the classic votive candle with grace. Arrange multiples along a sideboard, mantel, or coffee table for a twinkling highlight.

Materials for 1 votive jacket:
round clear-glass votive candle holder (no taller than 2" high)
scrap of posterboard
2"-wide wire mesh ribbon with wired edges: gold or silver
hot-glue gun and glue sticks
dried materials: bay leaves and/or lemon slices
Rub 'n Buff wax finish: gold or silver
¾ yard (⅛"-wide) ribbon: gold-and-silver or sage green-and-gold (optional)
3-mm gold or silver beads (optional)

Note: Do not leave burning candle unattended. For information on drying lemon slices, see page 72. For information on ordering dried bay leaves, see the box on page 151 and the source listing on page 152.

Measure circumference of candle holder and add ½". Cut a ½"-wide strip of posterboard and a length of wire mesh ribbon to this length. Hot-glue ends of posterboard strip together to form a circle, overlapping ends ¼". (Circle should fit loosely around candle holder.) Aligning 1 long edge of ribbon with bottom of posterboard base, glue ribbon to base, overlapping and gluing ends of ribbon.

Following manufacturer's directions, lightly apply gold or silver wax finish to front of bay leaves. Let dry.

For bay-leaf votive, referring to photograph, glue bay leaves on mesh ribbon jacket as desired. If desired, tie a 6-loop bow with ⅛"-wide ribbon and glue to bay leaves.

For lemon-slice votive, cut lemon slice in half. Repeat for number of slices needed to cover jacket. Aligning cut edge of slice with bottom edge of jacket, glue slices in place. Overlapping ends of leaves slightly, glue small bay leaves to bottom edge of lemon slices.

If desired, glue beads around top edge of jacket.

Weave a Welcoming Wreath

Strips of fabric come together to create a latticework wreath. To make it quickly, use your rotary cutter to cut the fabric strips as well as the prairie-point squares used for the decorative edging.

Materials:
½ yard (45"-wide) dark green cotton print
½ yard (45"-wide) light green cotton print
1 yard (36"-wide) fusible interfacing
rotary cutter, mat, and ruler (optional)
tissue paper
pushpin
10" length of string
2 (17") squares of thick batting
15" (¼"-wide) red corded piping
¼ yard (45"-wide) red print for bow
thread to match fabrics
15 (¼") red wooden beads
¾" plastic curtain ring

Note: Finished wreath is 15" in diameter. Seam allowance is ¼".

From dark green print, cut 1 (17") square for front and 1 (17") square for back. From light green print, cut 1 (17") square for front. From interfacing, cut 2 (17") squares and 1 (18") square.

Following manufacturer's instructions, fuse 1 (17") square of interfacing to wrong side of 17" dark green square. Repeat for light green square. Using rotary cutter and mat if desired, cut fused squares into 1"-wide strips.

Place 18" square of interfacing on work surface with fusible side up. Beginning and ending ½" from edges of square, lay dark green strips side by side vertically on interfacing, with edges touching. Pin ends of strips to interfacing. Weave light green strips horizontally over and under vertical strips. Pin ends of horizontal strips to interfacing. Following manufacturer's instructions, fuse strips in place. Remove pins. Trim excess interfacing from edges.

For wreath pattern, tape sheets of tissue paper together to form an 18" square. Referring to Diagram, fold square in half and then into fourths. Tie pushpin to 1 end of string. Tie other end of string to a pencil to make a compass with an 8" radius. Insert pushpin at folded corner of tissue. Holding string taut, draw an arc with an 8" radius. Draw a second arc with a 2" radius in the same manner. Cut along drawn lines through all layers. Unfold pattern.

Using pattern, cut out woven front, back, and 2 layers of batting. Staystitch ⅛" from inner and outer edges of woven front. Pin and baste 1 piece of batting to wrong side of woven front and 1 piece to wrong side of wreath back.

To make prairie points, cut 32 (2") squares from remaining dark green print. Fold squares in half diagonally. Fold in half again and press. With raw edges aligned and points toward center, pin prairie points

to right side of wreath front around outer edge, overlapping ends slightly. Position points so that folds of triangles face the same direction. Baste.

With raw edges aligned, baste piping to inner circle of wreath front. With right sides facing and raw edges aligned, stitch outer edge of wreath front to wreath back, leaving an opening for turning. Clip seam allowance to staystitching and turn. Slipstitch opening closed. Turn raw edges of inner circle under ¼" and slipstitch closed.

Tack beads to wreath front as desired.

For bow, from red print, cut 1 (10" x 44") strip and 1 (5") square. With right sides facing, fold strip in half lengthwise. Stitch along raw edges, stitching ends to a point and leaving an opening for turning. Turn and slipstitch opening closed. Press. With ends of strip matching, fold strip to make 2 loops of bow. For center band, with right sides facing, fold 5" square in half. Stitch along long edge; then turn and press with seam centered. Wrap band (seam side down) around center of bow. Whipstitch ends of band together. Tack bow to bottom front of wreath. To hang, tack curtain ring to top center back of wreath.

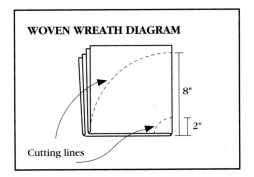

WOVEN WREATH DIAGRAM

8"

2"

Cutting lines

Fabric Alternatives

This woven fabric wreath has many options for exciting color and design combinations. Go romantic by substituting 1"-wide satin, velveteen, or grosgrain ribbon for the fabric strips, and add mother-of-pearl buttons in lieu of the beads. Consider striking color combinations like mauve and ivory, beige and white, or purple and gold. For a folk-art look, use strips of bright felt or wool and primary-color buttons. Or weave lengths of contrasting plaid ribbons for a tartan-style wreath.

Ideas

Outdoor Decor, Naturally

Once you've decked the halls, bring that greenery back outdoors to say welcome to all. Go beyond a wreath on the front door and decorate windows, the mailbox—even the garden gate!

Right: The mailbox is often the first thing people see as they arrive at your home; decorate it well. Fresh greenery, citrus fruit, pinecones, and artichokes cover this mailbox; the wire-edged ribbon bow will keep its shape despite the winter weather. If desired, your arrangement can be attached to a purchased mailbox frame (see the source listing on page 152).

Keep Your Arrangements Fresh as All Outdoors

Creating appealing designs from greenery and other natural materials requires only a little imagination and preparation. Follow these tips from florists to prolong the fresh beauty of your arrangements:

• To prepare greenery, cut stems at a slant and soak them in tepid water overnight in a cool place. Ivy and boxwood benefit from complete submersion in the water. You can also freshen juniper, pine, arborvitae, and fir by submerging them for one hour in warm water.

• If you live in a mild climate, you may want to add fresh flowers to your arrangement. Place the stems of fresh flowers in water-filled florist's picks. Check the picks every few days and refill them as needed.

• To bring out the natural luster of magnolia leaves, rub them with a soft cloth saturated with liquid floor wax.

• To reduce moisture loss, mist arrangements periodically with water or floral preservative.

Left: Diana Hansen of Birmingham, Alabama, greets her guests with a burst of tulips, paperwhites, and stars of Bethlehem tied to a base of bleached honeysuckle. She secures the flower stems in water-filled florist's picks, ensuring that they'll last for several days in mild temperatures.

Top right: For a nontraditional arrangement, Pam and Paul Jones of Rutledge, Georgia, add a spray of variegated holly, pine, and ribbon to this antique sled for a nostalgic display.

Bottom right: The Historic Fredericksburg Foundation in Virginia turns a barren winter window box into a lush showpiece with magnolia leaves, nandina berries, and mushrooms. Boxwood sprigs held in place with beeswax imitate the inviting look of candles in the window.

Information on vinegar painting and instructions for making the frame are on pages 42–43.

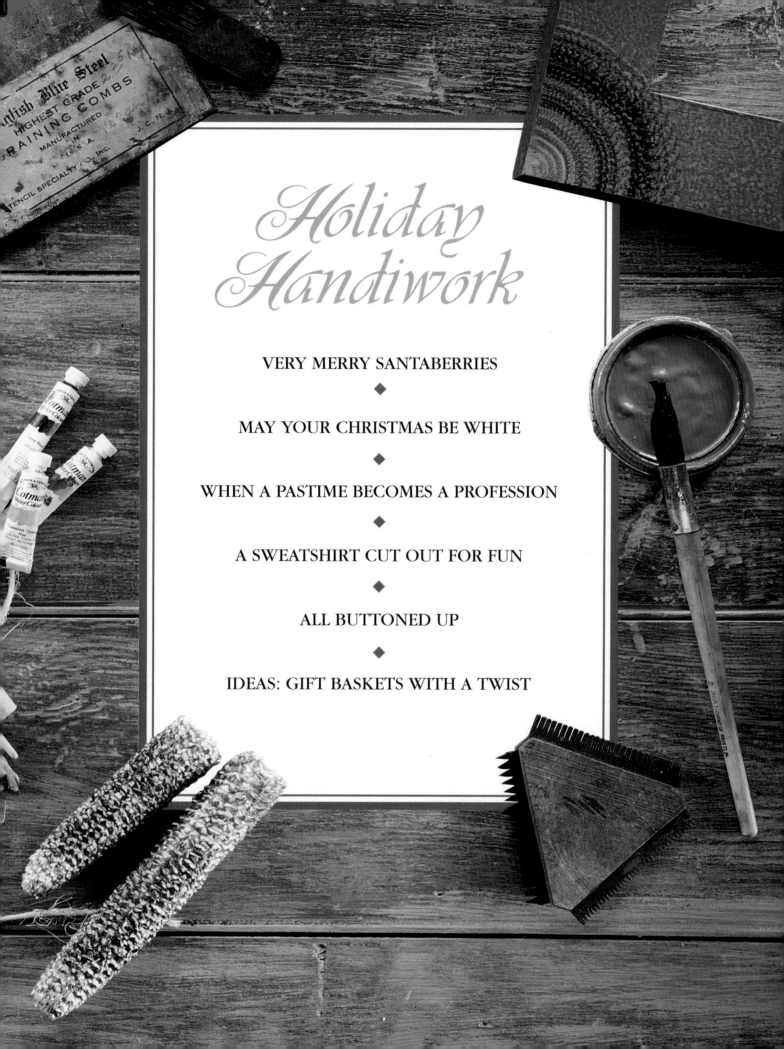

Holiday Handiwork

VERY MERRY SANTABERRIES

◆

MAY YOUR CHRISTMAS BE WHITE

◆

WHEN A PASTIME BECOMES A PROFESSION

◆

A SWEATSHIRT CUT OUT FOR FUN

◆

ALL BUTTONED UP

◆

IDEAS: GIFT BASKETS WITH A TWIST

Very Merry Santaberries

These jovial little Santas are sure to catch a smile! Animate this sweet wall hanging with a gathering of Santaberries nearby. The ornaments are stitched so quickly that they are perfect for small gifts—tuck them into a stocking or glue pin backs to small Santaberries to make little pins.

Wall Hanging

Materials:
patterns on page 132
tracing paper
¼ yard (45"-wide) dark green cotton print
¼ yard (45"-wide) muslin
⅜ yard (45"-wide) dark green cotton flannel
½ yard (45"-wide) red plaid cotton fabric
½ yard of thin batting
scraps of assorted red cotton prints
⅛ yard (45"-wide) pink cotton fabric
⅛ yard (45"-wide) black cotton fabric
thread to match fabrics
black fine-tipped permanent marker
white embroidery floss
size 3 embroidery needle
2 (¾") plastic curtain rings

Note: Finished size is 16" x 20". All seam allowances are ¼". Triangle patterns include ¼" seam allowance. Add ¼" seam allowance to appliqué pieces.

Using tracing paper, transfer triangle patterns to green print and cut 10 triangle As, 4 triangle Bs, and 6 (3½") squares for top. From muslin, cut 12 (3½") squares for top. From green flannel, cut 1 (12¾" x 17") rectangle for backing. From red plaid, cut 2 (16½" x 20½") rectangles for background. From batting, cut 1 (16½" x 20½") rectangle.

Following Diagram on page 30, with right sides facing and raw edges aligned, join squares and triangles into diagonal rows. Stitch rows together to form top.

For Santa appliqués, transfer patterns for Medium Santa to fabrics as indicated and cut 12 of each piece, adding ¼" seam allowances. Turn edge of appliqué pieces under ¼" and press. Using matching thread, hand-appliqué pieces to muslin squares in the following order: boots, body, beard, face. Using permanent marker, draw 2 dots for eyes.

With right sides facing and raw edges aligned, stitch finished top to green flannel, leaving an opening for turning. Clip corners and turn. Slip-stitch opening closed.

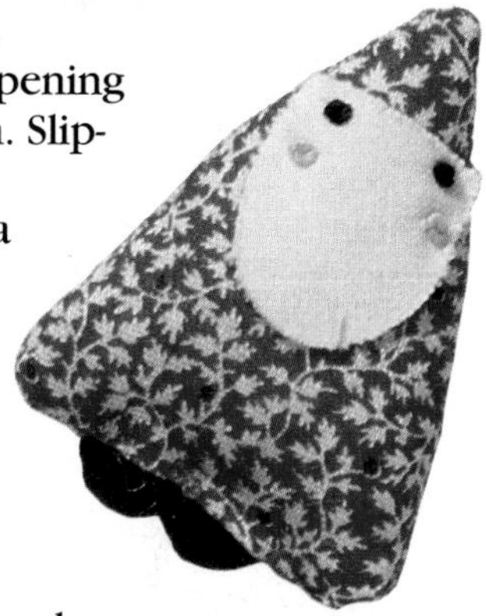

Using 6 strands of floss, make a knot at tip of each Santa hat and at top corner of green print squares as follows: Take a small stitch through fabric. Knot thread against fabric and trim ends to 1". Set pieced top aside.

For background, stack batting, red plaid top (right side up), and red plaid backing (right side down). Baste. Stitch through all layers along outside edges, leaving an opening for turning. Clip corners, trim excess fabric and batting from seams, and turn. Slipstitch opening closed.

Center pieced top on background; then tack to background at 3 points along top edge.

To hang finished piece, on back of background, position curtain rings 1½" from top edge and stitch in place.

Ornaments

Materials for 1 ornament:
patterns on page 132
tracing paper
scrap of red cotton print
thread to match fabric
small amount of polyester stuffing
scraps of felt: black or brown for boots; white and light pink for face and beard
scrap of muslin
embroidery floss: black, pink, white
size 3 embroidery needle
2 black seed beads (optional)

Note: Add ¼" seam allowance to pattern pieces as directed in following instructions.

To make Santa, with right sides facing, fold red

cotton in half. Using tracing paper, transfer desired body pattern and markings to top layer of cotton. Machine-stitch along outline through both layers, leaving open where indicated. Cut out body, adding ¼" seam allowance. Clip curves and corners and turn. Stuff. Transfer boots pattern to black or brown felt (do not add seam allowance) and cut out. Referring to pattern, slip top of boots into body opening; then slipstitch opening closed.

To make face and beard, for large Santa, fold scrap of muslin in half and repeat steps for body, stitching completely around beard. Make a slash in back layer only of beard and turn beard through slash. Slipstitch opening closed and press. Using white thread, topstitch around beard, ⅛" from edge. For medium Santa, transfer beard and face patterns to felt as indicated (do not add seam allowance) and cut out. For small Santa, transfer beard pattern to muslin (do not add seam allowance) and cut out.

To attach face and beard: For large Santa, referring to pattern, position beard on body. Using 6 strands of black floss, embroider French knots for eyes, stitching through layers of beard to catch body fabric. Using 6 strands of pink floss, embroider cross-stitches for cheeks. Repeat for small Santa, substituting French knots for cheeks. For medium Santa, position face on top of beard and position on body. Stitch to body with black French knots for eyes. Or, if desired, stitch 2 seed beads in place for eyes.

If desired, make a knot at top of hat as follows: Using 6 strands of white floss, take a tiny stitch through tip of hat. Knot thread against fabric and trim ends to 1".

For hanger, thread needle with 2 (6") strands of floss and stitch through top back of head. Knot ends together to make a loop.

SANTABERRY WALL HANGING—
Constructing Quilt Top

Fashion a Fine Humpty Dumpty

*Dressed in his Christmas best, this nursery rhyme character
will delight little ones of all ages. Luckily, he won't crack if he takes
a great fall—careful stitching and soft stuffing ensure a safe landing.*

Materials:
patterns on pages 138–39
tracing paper
¼ yard (45"-wide) prequilted unbleached muslin
¼ yard (45"-wide) prequilted red print fabric
thread to match fabrics
2 (size 1) black snaps
1 (³⁄₁₆") black shank button
cosmetic powder blush
water-soluble marker
polyester stuffing
⅛ yard (45"-wide) black cotton
¼ yard (45"-wide) white cotton
⅛ yard (45"-wide) green calico

Note: Patterns include ¼" seam allowances.

Using tracing paper, transfer patterns for head, body, and legs to fabrics and cut out.

With right sides facing and raw edges aligned, stitch 2 head pieces together along center seam for front. Staystitch along lower edge. Repeat to make head back.

With right sides facing and raw edges aligned, stitch 2 body pieces together along center seam for front. Staystitch across upper edge. Repeat to make body back.

With right sides facing, raw edges aligned, and center front seams matching, stitch head front to body front along staystitched edges. Repeat to make back.

Referring to pattern for facial features and using black thread, attach top halves of snaps for eyes and button for nose on head front. Using red thread and a small running stitch, outline cheeks and mouth. Lightly shade cheeks with blush.

For sleeves, from prequilted red print, cut 2 (4⅝" x 5¾") rectangles. For hands, from prequilted muslin, cut 2 (4⅝" x 2¼") rectangles.

For arms, with right sides facing and raw edges aligned, stitch 1 sleeve piece to 1 hand piece along 4⅝" edge. With right sides facing, fold sleeve/hand piece in half lengthwise. Using water-soluble marker, transfer hand pattern to hand piece with thumb toward long open edge. Referring to pattern and beginning at folded edge where hand joins sleeve, stitch along outline of hand in direction indicated. Continue to stitch sleeve, leaving top open. Trim excess seam allowance on hand, clip curves, and turn. Stuff arm firmly to within 2" of top edge; stitch top edge closed. Repeat for other arm.

With right sides facing and raw edges aligned, stitch 2 leg pieces together, leaving top open. Clip curves and turn. Stuff leg firmly to within 1½" of top edge. Using a gathering stitch, stitch top edge of leg together, matching front and back seams. Repeat for other leg.

With raw edges aligned and toes pointing toward head, baste legs to body front ¼" on either side of center seam.

With right sides facing, raw edges aligned, and legs inside, stitch body front to body back, matching center seams and leaving an opening for turning. Clip curves and turn. Stuff body firmly; then whipstitch opening closed.

Align 1 arm along 1 side seam of body, with top of arm covering middle seam of body. Stitch arm securely to body. Repeat for other arm.

For stand-up collar, from white cotton, cut a 5" x 19" strip. With right sides facing, fold strip in half lengthwise. Stitch across short ends; turn and press. Place collar around middle of doll, with raw edge ¾" below middle seam and ends overlapping slightly at center front seam. Using long running stitches, stitch collar to body. Fold down points of collar and press.

For tie, from green calico, cut 1 (3½" x 19") strip and 1 (3½" x 26") strip. With right sides facing, fold 1 strip in half lengthwise and stitch along long open edge and 1 end. Turn and press. Slipstitch opening closed. Repeat for other strip. Place 19"-long strip around middle of body, covering raw edge of collar and overlapping ends at center front. Tack ends to body. Tie remaining strip in a bow and tack to center front over green band.

On, Dasher!

Who wouldn't like to speed through the night with one of Saint Nick's reindeer? These clever children in cross-stitch have persuaded Santa to let them take Dasher on a ride through the snow.

Materials:
chart and color key on page 133
12½" x 14" piece of 14-count white
   Aida cloth
size 24 tapestry needle
embroidery floss (see color key)

Note: Finished design is 6½" x 8".

Using 3 strands of floss and stitching over 1 thread, center and work cross-stitch design on Aida according to chart.

Frame as desired. (Finished project is shown in a 8½" x 10" wooden frame.)

May Your Christmas Be White

It's the color of Santa's beard, angels' wings, and snow: White says "Christmas" almost as much as red and green. Like the wreath below, these projects are perfect for dressing your home in winter white.

Woolly Wreath

Materials:
1 yard (60"-wide) imitation lambswool
ecru sewing thread
14"-diameter Styrofoam wreath
craft glue
ecru embroidery floss
74 mother-of-pearl buttons in assorted sizes

Note: Finished wreath is 18" in diameter. All seam allowances are ¼".

From lambswool, cut 2 (15" x 60") strips. With right sides facing, stitch strips together at 1 end to form 1 long strip. With right sides facing, fold strip in half lengthwise and stitch along long edge to form a tube. Turn.

With a serrated knife, cut Styrofoam wreath in half. Insert 1 half of wreath into lambswool tube, gathering lambswool to form folds. Apply glue to 1 cut end of wreath, holding fabric away from glue. Glue to 1 end of other half of wreath; pin to hold until glue dries. Slide lambswool tube around wreath to expose remaining cut ends of wreath. Glue remaining ends together, pinning to hold until glue dries.

Turn raw ends of lambswool tube under; slipstitch opening closed.

With 6 strands of floss, stitch 1 button to wreath front, leaving 1" tails on top of button. Knot tails, pulling knot tightly against button to secure. Repeat to attach remaining buttons to wreath as desired.

For hanger, stitch a 10" length of 6-strand floss through top back of wreath; knot ends to make a loop.

Woolly Stocking

Materials:
pattern on page 134
tracing paper
⅓ yard (60"-wide) imitation lambswool
ecru sewing thread
ecru embroidery floss
35 mother-of-pearl buttons in assorted sizes

Fold lambswool in half with right sides facing. Using tracing paper, enlarge and transfer pattern to wrong side of top layer of lambswool. Stitch along outline through both layers, leaving top open. Cut out ¼" from stitching line. Clip curves and turn.

Turn top raw edge under ½" and slipstitch hem.

With 6 strands of floss, stitch 1 button to stocking front, leaving 1" tails on top of button. Knot tails, pulling knot tightly against button to secure. Repeat to attach remaining buttons, reserving 1 large button for hanger.

For hanger, stitch a 12" length of 6-strand floss through upper left corner of stocking. Pass thread through remaining large button and knot to secure button 3" from stocking. Knot ends to make a loop.

Woolly Birds

Materials for 1 bird:
patterns on page 135
tracing paper
scrap of imitation lambswool
ecru sewing thread
polyester stuffing
1 (½") mother-of-pearl button

Left and above: The simple addition of mother-of-pearl buttons gives the rough-hewn lambswool charm. For information on collecting vintage buttons, see page 50; to order buttons in bulk, see page 152.

Fold lambswool in half with right sides facing. Using tracing paper, transfer patterns to wrong side of top layer of lambswool. Stitch along outline through both layers, leaving open as indicated. Cut out ¼" from stitching line. Clip curves and corners and turn. Stuff body with a small amount of stuffing; do not stuff wing. Slipstitch openings closed.

Referring to pattern, position wing on body and pin; then position button on wing. To attach wing, using doubled thread, insert needle through button and stitch back and forth through all layers several times. Knot thread on back of bird.

For hanger, stitch an 8" length of thread through top of body; knot ends to make a loop.

Paper Heart Garlands

Materials:
patterns on page 135
tracing paper
cream 8½" x 11" medium-weight paper
craft knife
craft glue

Note: Each sheet of paper yields 6 large hearts or 12 small hearts.

Referring to Diagram 1, measure and mark 1 sheet of paper into rectangles, following black lines to make 6 large hearts, and following both black and gray lines to make 12 small hearts. Cut along drawn lines. Repeat to make as many rectangles as you will need hearts for desired length of garland.

Fold 1 rectangle in half lengthwise and make a sharp crease. Transfer pattern and markings for desired heart onto folded rectangle. With scissors, cut out along top curve; using craft knife, cut center slit. Open heart. Referring to Diagram 2, overlap outside strips at center and glue in place. Repeat for remaining hearts.

To construct garland, spread glue over bottom third of 1 heart front. Overlap another heart on top and press. Continue gluing and overlapping hearts until garland is desired length. If desired, make arched garlands by angling each heart slightly before gluing it in place. For bottom heart of garland, trim end to form point.

Above: Ten of these quick-to-cut paper hearts make up each arch on the door front, and about twenty large hearts compose each graceful swag.

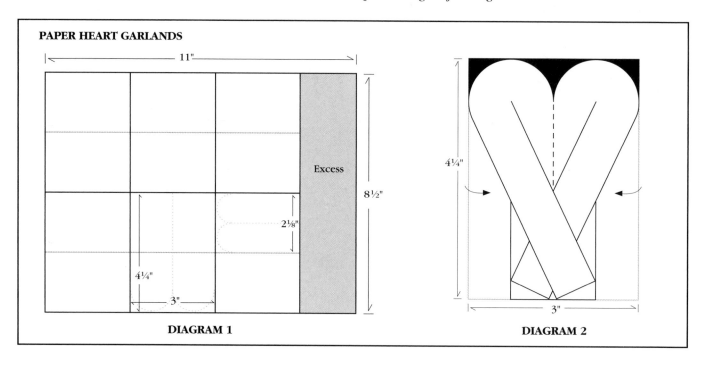

PAPER HEART GARLANDS

11"

8½"

Excess

2⅛"

4¼"

3"

DIAGRAM 1

4¼"

3"

DIAGRAM 2

36

Trio of Angels

Materials:
patterns on page 136
tracing paper
1 (12" x 18") sheet of white card-stock paper
scrap of gold metallic paper
craft knife
craft glue
1 (6" x 9½") envelope

Transfer angel pattern to tracing paper and cut out. From card stock, measure and cut a 17⅛" x 8½" rectangle. Fold rectangle accordion-style into thirds to make a 5¹¹⁄₁₆" x 8½" rectangle. Aligning fold line of pattern along folded edge of top layer of card, lightly transfer outline, interior of halo, and neck of angel to card stock with pencil. Using craft knife, cut out through all layers.

Open card. Transfer arm pattern for left and right angels and arms and mouth for center angel to card and cut out. Gently erase any pencil lines. Transfer horn and book pattern to metallic paper and cut out 2 horns and 1 book. Glue horns and book to appropriate angels (see photograph). Let dry.

If desired, sign greeting on right-hand angel. Insert card in envelope to send.

Below: Send this host of angels as a greeting card; your friend can use it as a decoration for Christmases to come.

37

Stack Spools for a Sweet Shelf

The spindles of this classic design are accented with wooden spools, just like the ones saved in many a sewing basket. It's the ideal place to showcase miniatures collections such as Christmas angels, prized thimbles, or antique trinkets.

Materials:
patterns on page 146
tracing paper
1 (3" x 20") piece of ½"-thick dressed pine
band saw or jigsaw
handsaw
1 (4" x 52") piece of ½"-thick dressed pine
sandpaper: 100 grit, 150 grit
electric drill with ⅛" bit
2 (36") lengths of ⅛"-diameter wooden dowels
wood glue
54 (⅞" x 1⅛"-high) wooden spools
8 (#4) finishing nails
2 (2¼") sawtooth picture hangers
semigloss spray varnish

Note: Dressed pine is wood that has been thinned with a wood plane to desired thickness.

Using tracing paper, transfer back piece patterns to ends of 3"-wide pine as indicated. Using band saw or jigsaw, cut out. Set back piece aside.

Using handsaw, cut 4"-wide pine into 2 (16") lengths, 1 (12") length, and 1 (8") length for shelves A–D (see Diagram). Beginning with 100-grit sandpaper and finishing with 150 grit, sand edges of shelves and back piece smooth.

To mark drilling holes for dowel placement: For Shelf A, measure ¾" from end of shelf and mark a line parallel to end. Mark center of this line. Then mark 1¼" on each side of center mark along drawn line. Repeat to mark other end of Shelf A and bottom of Shelf B.

On top of Shelf B, measure 2¾" from each end and mark as described above.

On bottom of Shelf C, measure ¾" from each end and mark as described above.

On top of Shelf C, measure 2¾" from each end and mark as described above.

On bottom of Shelf D, measure ¾" from each end and mark as described above.

At each mark, drill a ¼"-deep hole. Erase pencil marks.

Using handsaw, cut each dowel into 9 (4") lengths, for a total of 18 (4") dowels.

Glue 1 dowel into each hole on Shelf A. Thread 3 spools onto each dowel, gluing each spool. On bottom of Shelf B, drop a small amount of glue into each hole; turn shelf over and lay shelf on top of dowels, inserting dowels firmly into holes. Referring to Diagram for placement, repeat to assemble remaining shelves.

Stand entire unit up and weight by placing a heavy object on top shelf until glue dries.

Lay shelf unit flat. Center back piece on shelf unit (see Diagram) and attach with finishing nails. On back of back piece, nail a picture hanger 5" from each end.

Spray entire unit with 2 coats of varnish, allowing varnish to dry between applications.

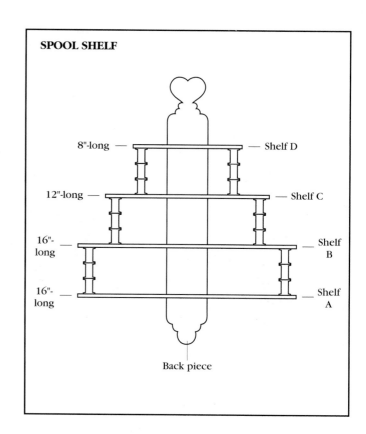

SPOOL SHELF

8"-long — — Shelf D

12"-long — — Shelf C

16"-long — — Shelf B

16"-long — — Shelf A

Back piece

When a Pastime Becomes a Profession

"Follow your heart," goes the quip, "and the money will follow."
Happily, this is exactly what happened to Rebecca A. Erb, a
Pennsylvania crafter whose hobby—vinegar painting—has
grown into a richly satisfying business.

Rebecca most savors her success during Christmas, when being her own boss frees her to schedule time for favorite traditions—cutting rose hips for decorations, making homemade cider and cookies, and hosting a holiday open house. She attributes her good fortune to a love of the craft and plain old good luck. But she has also made some smart choices on the long path from pastime to profession.

When she was a girl, Rebecca tried many different crafts. "My great-grandfather was a basket-weaver," says Rebecca, "and my grandmother and mother were quilters, so handcrafts definitely run in my family." In fact, Rebecca's grandmother helped with her very first project—a pillowcase embellished with redwork embroidery.

Later, Rebecca learned to sew, and she made teddy bears with movable arms and legs. By 1980, she was back into embroidery, stitching samplers based on historic designs. "Looking back," Rebecca says, "I can see I was still searching for my niche, for my special talent."

But matters took a lucky turn. Rebecca had seen antique samplers displayed in their original vinegar-grained frames, and she had always thought that similar frames would perfectly set off her own samplers. So she enrolled in a one-day course on vinegar painting and learned the basics.

"I loved it!" Rebecca remembers. She began making frames, and when they sold out at a local craft show, people began asking her to make more. "I realized that my hobby could be a small business," she says. "I thought about it and thought about it, and meanwhile I continued taking orders for the frames. Once I had a backlog of a couple of dozen orders, I quit my office job and went for it."

Rebecca made several smart decisions that ensured her move was a successful one. She developed a line of hand-painted pieces that run the gamut from small and simple to large and intricate—a line that appeals to all tastes and budgets. She then began selling her pieces at the myriad craft and antiques shows for which central Pennsylvania has become famous. Her favorites are the holiday craft fairs, events made entertaining by all of the festive

Right: During the cold winter months, Rebecca works hard to get ready for the holiday craft shows. Her most popular pieces are vinegar-painted Shaker boxes, miniature chests, and picture frames in vibrant colors and energetic patterns. (For a source listing, see page 152.) For more on vinegar painting and to learn how to make the red frame at center, see pages 42–43.

Left: Although vinegar painting remains her favorite pursuit, Rebecca's newest avocation is rug hooking. The lamb design hanging over the mantel was her first project; the woolly-bearded Santa is her latest.

40

decorations and the large, cheerful crowds.

But perhaps her smartest move was to submit her work for inclusion in the Pennsylvania Guild of Craftsmen. To her delight, she was readily granted admission. Since then, honors have also come from national magazines that include Rebecca in their surveys of today's finest American craftspeople.

Rebecca is quick to credit her family with her success. Daughters Christie and Amy don't mind the times when their mother, who sometimes finds the basement too remote, sets up operations on the kitchen table instead. And Rebecca's husband, Bill, gladly contributes his woodworking skills and genially makes his way around the chaos that inevitably attends a business run out of the home. "My family has been instrumental in the success of my business," stresses Rebecca. "When they come home

and find something in the oven, it's rarely supper."

These days, what they're likely to find in the oven is a mound of recently dyed wool. Rebecca's newest hobby is rug hooking, and she goes about it in her typically thorough fashion—dyeing her own wool, heat-setting it in the oven, and then cutting it in strips for the next project. Last Christmas, along with the pieces she usually vinegar-paints to give to family members, she also hooked for her mother a design based on the Carolina Lily, her mother's favorite quilt pattern.

But for the time being, this is one pastime that won't metamorphose into a profession. "Rug hooking is something I want to do at the end of the day, when I'm ready to relax," Rebecca says. "When I wake up in the morning fresh and full of energy, I always turn to vinegar painting first."

Vinegar Painting: The Easy Basics

Vinegar painting offers dramatic effects with little effort. Here, Rebecca A. Erb, a master of the technique, shares her secrets and shows you how to make a boldly patterned frame. (For more on Rebecca and a photograph of the finished frame, see pages 40–41.)

Rebecca is always happy to point out the charms of vinegar painting. One is that it is surprisingly easy. You simply cover a painted surface with a vinegar-and-paint mixture and then imprint a design in the mixture.

Another charm is its forgiveness. At any time before you varnish the piece, if you aren't pleased with its design, you simply wipe it off with vinegar and begin anew.

Over the years, vinegar painters have freely modified both the technique and the actual recipe for the paint. Rebecca jokes that there are as many vinegar-paint recipes as there are vinegar painters.

Many formulas call for blending tempera powder paint with a mixture of vinegar, sugar, and liquid soap. Rebecca gets terrific results using the simplest of recipes: one (eight-milliliter) tube of watercolor paint mixed with a teaspoon of vinegar.

The tempera-paint formula certainly works, but Rebecca prefers using watercolor paints because she feels they are a bit richer in color and come in a wider palette.

An *oil-based* paint is always used as a base coat for vinegar paint. For best results, use dark vinegar paint over a light base coat. Two of Rebecca's favorite combinations are burnt sienna over antique yellow and black over slate blue.

Rebecca is also fond of using more than one color of vinegar paint in a single design. The same principle of dark over light works here, too, she says—just apply the lightest vinegar paint first and the darkest color last.

You can use almost anything to imprint your design in the vinegar paint. Crumpled paper, a comb, or a dried corncob works well. You can even use your hands—the side of your fist, your palm, and your fingertips can create intriguing patterns.

Rebecca says this is one craft in which you can afford to be adventuresome. After all, if a design you envisioned as daring ends up looking like one big mess, you can always wipe it off with vinegar and try again.

Painting a Frame

To make your own frame, begin with an unfinished, preferably flat wooden frame. (For handmade frames, see the source listing on page 152.) Sand the frame with 150-grit sandpaper. If desired, apply a clear wood primer and let it dry.

Apply an oil-based paint as a base coat and let it

Painting Against the Grain

During the 19th century, American craftsmen were scrambling to keep up with the demand for "fancy graining" on woodwork and furniture. Using paint and a deft hand, they could make simple furniture look as if it were fashioned from the very finest wood, and they had no shortage of customers.

The painters got busy devising different faux finishes, one of which was vinegar painting, or "vinegar graining," as it's sometimes called. Vividly colored, vigorously patterned vinegar painting was a wild caricature compared to the amazingly realistic effects achieved by master grainers, but it was quick, easy, and inexpensive. Country craftsmen in particular embraced the new technique.

Today, folk art and primitive pieces are popular, and the irony is that the vinegar-painted pieces are often more appealing than the expertly grained pieces they are meant to imitate. And the technique itself is being given new life by craftspeople who are discovering what the 19th-century painters knew—not only is vinegar painting economical, but it is also great fun.

Step 1: Mixing about four parts watercolor paint to one part vinegar, make a light vinegar paint and a dark vinegar paint. Using a medium paintbrush, apply the light vinegar paint over the base coat.

Step 3: While the light vinegar paint is still wet, use a narrower paintbrush to apply the dark vinegar paint last. In each corner of the frame, dab on the paint in a pattern similar to that shown above.

Step 2: Dab a damp sponge into the light vinegar paint to create a mottled effect.

Step 4: Using a dried corncob, blend the dark vinegar paint to create a fan design in each corner. Hold one end stationary against the outside corner of the frame, moving the other end up and down to blend the paint. After the paint dries, apply two coats of semigloss polyurethane varnish, letting varnish dry between coats.

dry. (For the frame shown here, Rebecca used old gold flat oil-based paint.) Sand the frame lightly. Apply a second coat of paint and let it dry.

Wipe the frame with a sponge or cloth soaked in white or cider vinegar. Sand the frame lightly, taking care not to sand the paint off the edges. Repeat these two steps—probably two or three times—until the vinegar no longer beads up. Remove traces of vinegar with a damp sponge.

Now begins the fun of patterning the frame.

The above photographs show in detail how Rebecca created her vivid design with only two colors of vinegar paint. For the light color, Rebecca mixed one tube of alizarin crimson watercolor paint with one teaspoon of vinegar. Since she needed less of the dark color, she mixed a quarter of a tube of dark green watercolor paint with a quarter teaspoon of vinegar.

A Treasure of a Chest

Attention to detail makes this a piece to be cherished. To construct it, you need only basic woodworking skills (you could also purchase an unfinished chest). To finish it, use the time-honored art of vinegar painting. For more on this technique, see pages 42–43.

Constructing the Chest

Materials:
1 (6-foot) pine 1 x 12
table saw or ripsaw
handsaw or skill saw
electric drill with ⁵⁄₆₄" bit
24 (1⁵⁄₈") drywall screws
flathead screwdriver
¾" plywood: 1 (11³⁄₁₆" x 22³⁄₁₆") piece for lid, 1 (9½" x 20½") piece for bottom, 1 (1³⁄₁₆" x 48") for furring strip
#4 finishing nails
wood glue
48"-long wood moldings: 1 (1³⁄₁₆"-wide) teardrop doorstop molding, 1 (¹¹⁄₁₆"-wide) cove molding, and 1 (1⁷⁄₁₆"-wide) panel molding
miter saw and miter box
wood filler
2 (2" x 1⁹⁄₁₆") butt hinges with screws
sandpaper: 120-grit, 360-grit

Note: Finished chest is 24" x 12" x 11¼".

Using table saw or ripsaw, cut pine 1 x 12 to a 10½" width. Using handsaw, cut pine into the following lengths: 2 (22") pieces for front and back and 2 (9½") pieces for sides. Label all pieces. Stack matching pieces together to make sure they are the same size. Trim as necessary.

Referring to Diagram 1 on page 46, position 1 side piece to abut 1 end of front piece.

Referring to Diagram 2, mark 3 drilling holes at bottom of front piece: Measure 1½" from bottom and make a mark. Measure 1½" from first mark and make a second mark. Measure halfway between these 2 marks and make a third mark. Drill holes at each mark. Repeat at top of front piece as indicated. Screw front piece to side piece. Repeat to attach remaining side and back piece.

Turn chest upside down. To attach bottom piece, position 9½" x 20½" piece of plywood in bottom of chest. If too tight, sand as needed to make it fit. Recess bottom piece ¼" in bottom of chest. Using finishing nails, nail through sides, front, and back of chest to secure bottom.

From 1³⁄₁₆" x 48" plywood furring strip, cut 1 (22") length for front and 2 (11⁵⁄₈") lengths for sides. Referring to Diagram 3, align 22" strip with bottom edge of chest front. Using wood glue, glue strip to chest front. Reinforce with finishing nails. Repeat to attach side furring strips to chest.

To prepare moldings, cut each of the 3 moldings into the following lengths: 1 (24") piece for front and 2 (12") pieces for sides. Using miter saw and miter box, miter each 24" piece on both ends; miter each 12" piece on 1 end only, making sure that mitered ends for front and sides match. (When finished, molding will be mitered on front of chest, but will be flush with back of chest.)

To attach bottom molding, referring to Diagram 3, use wood glue to attach 24"-long teardrop molding to chest front on top of furring strip. Reinforce molding with finishing nails. Repeat to attach 12"-long teardrop molding to sides. Attach cove molding flush against top edge of furring strip on front and sides in same manner.

To attach lid molding, referring to Diagram 4, align top edge of 24"-long panel molding with top front edge of chest lid. Using wood glue and finishing nails, attach molding to chest lid. Repeat to attach side moldings.

To attach chest lid, on underneath side of back edge of chest lid, measure and mark 4⁷⁄₁₆" from each side of lid. On top edge of chest back piece, measure and mark 4¼" from each side. (Chest lid will overlap chest ³⁄₁₆" on each side.) Place 1 hinge over mark. Aligning center hole of hinge with mark, mark remaining holes. Repeat for other hinges. Remove hinges and drill holes at marks. Screw hinges to chest.

Fill all nail and screw holes with wood filler; let dry. Sand smooth with 360-grit sandpaper. Beginning with 120-grit sandpaper and finishing with 360 grit, sand edges and sides of chest smooth.

Painting the Chest

Materials:
1 quart of clear wood primer (optional)
1 quart of robin's egg blue semigloss oil-based
  paint
paintbrushes
white or cider vinegar
sugar
liquid soap
black tempera powder paint or 1 (8-ml) tube
  of black watercolor paint
disposable container with lid
newspaper
modeling clay
satin varnish

Following manufacturer's instructions, apply wood primer to inside and outside of chest if desired; let dry. Apply 1 coat of blue enamel to inside and outside of chest; let dry.

For tempera-paint recipe, combine ¼ cup vinegar, ½ teaspoon sugar, and 1 tablespoon liquid soap. In disposable container, measure 2 tablespoons tempera paint. Add enough vinegar mixture to make a thin wash, stirring until well blended. Keep vinegar paint covered when not in use.

For watercolor-paint recipe, mix 1 tube of watercolor paint with 1 teaspoon vinegar in disposable container, stirring until well blended.

Working in a small area at a time, use a soft paintbrush to apply vinegar paint. While paint is still wet, dab the area with a crumpled ball of newspaper to

give texture to chest. Repeat to cover entire outside of chest, including molding, with same texture.

To add sunflower motifs to chest, shape modeling clay into several 2" balls and several finger-sized "cigars." Referring to photograph for placement, reapply vinegar paint to working area for motif and then dab with crumpled newspaper. Press clay balls into paint to make center dot motif. Use clay cigars to make "petals." On top of chest, work 1 whole sunflower motif in center and ¼ motif in 4 corners (see photograph). Repeat for front and back of chest, working ¼ motif only in lower 2 corners. On sides of chest, work ¼ motif in lower 2 corners. Use a fresh piece of clay when clay gets too misshapen or soiled to make a good design.

If you are not pleased with an area, wipe it clean with a vinegar-soaked soft cloth, remove traces of vinegar with a damp sponge, and begin again.

Let finished chest dry. Apply 2 coats of satin varnish, letting dry between applications.

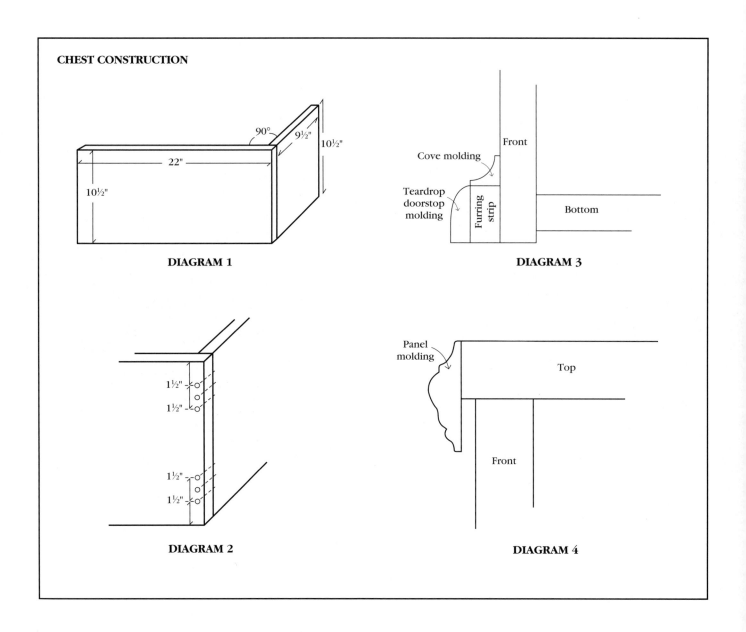

CHEST CONSTRUCTION

DIAGRAM 1

DIAGRAM 2

DIAGRAM 3

DIAGRAM 4

A Sweatshirt Cut Out for Fun

Delight a child on Christmas morning with this cozy sweatshirt. The design is a simple version of reverse appliqué: Just stitch the fabric to the inside of the sweatshirt and cut the design out of the front.

Materials:
pattern on page 137
tracing paper
¼ yard of green print fabric
1 child's white sweatshirt
thread: white, red
¼ yard of white sweatshirt fleece
liquid ravel preventer
30" (⅛"-wide) red satin ribbon
4 (⅜") gold star studs

Note: Prewash fabrics and sweatshirt before using. Enlarge tree pattern as desired to accommodate a larger-sized sweatshirt.

From green print, cut an 8" x 12" rectangle. Using tracing paper, center and transfer pattern onto wrong side of fabric rectangle; do not cut out.

Turn sweatshirt inside out and lay flat on table with front side up. With right side down, center green fabric rectangle on sweatshirt, with top of tree at least 1½" below neckline. Pin and baste in place along outer edge of rectangle. With white thread and using 16 stitches per inch, stitch along all lines of tree, being careful not to stitch through back of sweatshirt.

From sweatshirt fleece, cut an 8" x 12" rectangle. With right side down, position fleece rectangle over tree design; baste along outer edge of rectangle.

Turn sweatshirt right side out. Stitching over existing lines, stitch around outline of tree only to secure fleece, being careful not to stitch through back of sweatshirt. Remove all basting.

To create cutwork design, pull green fabric slightly away from top layer of sweatshirt. Make a small clip in center of top section of tree. Insert scissors into clip. Cut out top section of tree, cutting ⅛" *inside* stitching line and exposing green fabric. Repeat for remaining areas of tree.

Turn sweatshirt inside out. Trim away excess fleece and fabric from outside edges of design, cutting ¼" *outside* stitching line. Apply liquid ravel preventer to outer edge of fabric tree.

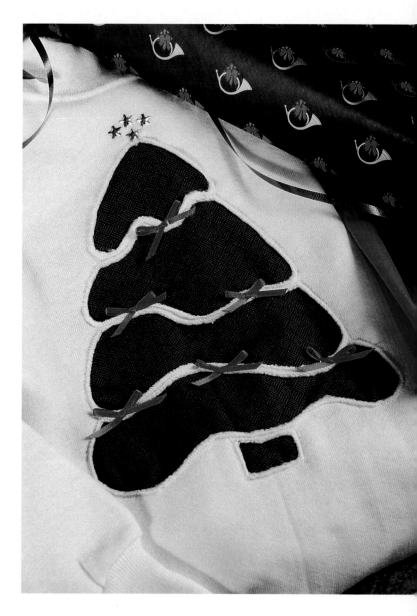

Cut ribbon into 6 (5") lengths. Apply liquid ravel preventer to cut ends of ribbon. Tie each length into a bow. Using red thread, tack bows to sweatshirt as indicated on pattern. Position star studs at top of tree and push studs into sweatshirt. Bend prongs to secure studs on sweatshirt.

Christmas Tree Sprites

With their winsome costumes and attentive air, these pixies seem poised to execute a pas de trois. *In Victorian times, ornaments like these were made of bisque and expensive laces, but this trio makes a virtue of such humble materials as muslin and upholstery cording.*

48

Materials for 1 sprite:
pattern on page 140
black marker
tracing paper
2 (6½" x 7½") pieces of muslin
brown fine-point permanent marker
acrylic paints: rose, white, blue, peach
fine-tipped paintbrush
thread: white, green
small amount of polyester stuffing
thin wooden dowel or crochet hook (for
stuffing tool)
12" length of ¼"-diameter twisted rayon
upholstery cording: light red (for
redheaded sprite), yellow (for blonde
sprite), or light brown (for brunette sprite)
hot-glue gun and glue sticks
pinking shears
4 yards of 6"-wide white fine-mesh net
1 branch of small polyester "silk" roses (for
redheaded and brunette sprites)
1 branch of ecru polyester "silk" hydrangea
(for blonde sprite)
1 branch of green-and-purple polyester "silk"
hydrangea (for brunette sprite)
1 branch of dark green polyester "silk" foliage
with leaves about 2" x 3" (see note below)

Note: All 3 sprites can be made with the amount of dark green polyester "silk" foliage listed above. If desired, practice tracing and painting faces on scraps of muslin before painting face on ornament. Finished size is 6½" tall.

Using black marker and tracing paper, trace pattern. Tape pattern to a light box or sunny window. Tape 1 muslin piece on top of pattern, centering pattern on fabric.

Using brown marker, trace outline of body on fabric (wrong side). Turn fabric over and retape on pattern, centering face within outline of head. Trace face on fabric (right side). Remove tape from fabric and pattern.

To paint face, paint lips rose. Mix white with blue to make light blue and dilute with water to make a semitransparent wash; paint "whites" of eyes. Fill in pupils with brown marker. If desired, mix white with peach to make pale peach and dilute with water to make a wash; paint cheeks. Let dry.

With right sides facing and raw edges aligned, pin fabric pieces together. Using white thread and 12 or more stitches per inch, hand- or machine-stitch along outline through both layers.

Cut out sprite, leaving a ⅛" seam allowance.

On back, slash fabric where indicated on pattern, taking care not to cut front. Clip curves and turn sprite through slash.

Stuff sprite gently but firmly, using dowel for hard-to-reach areas. Slipstitch opening closed.

Cut length of upholstery cording in half. Separate silky strands of rayon from coarse core material and discard core. Fluff rayon to create masses of curls. Position curls as desired on head and tack in place.

Bend arms at elbows and legs at knees to position them as desired. Secure each bend at the fold with a few stitches or a drop of glue.

Cross legs at ankles and secure with stitches or a drop of glue.

For skirt, use pinking shears to trim each long edge of net into a series of 1½"-deep points. Fold net in half lengthwise and run a gathering thread just inside fold. Pull to gather net to fit around sprite's waist. Position top edge of skirt just under sprite's arms and secure.

Disassemble branches of leaves and flowers. Remove and discard plastic veins from backs of leaves.

For redheaded sprite (left in photograph), select 4 large light green leaves, 7 small light green leaves, 1 small rosebud with 2"-long stem, and 2 dark green leaves. Referring to photograph for placement, glue large light green leaves around waist for overskirt; glue small light green leaves around shoulders for collar. For wings, fold large dark green leaves in half and glue bases of leaves to upper back of sprite. Tack stem of rosebud to 1 hand, pulling stitches to bend hand slightly inward.

For blonde sprite (center in photograph), select 16 ecru hydrangea blossoms and 2 large dark green leaves. Referring to photograph for placement, glue 10 blossoms around hem of skirt. For collar, remove plastic stamens from remaining blossoms; fold blossoms in half and glue around shoulders. For wings, glue leaves to body as described above for the redheaded sprite.

For brunette sprite (right in photograph), select 10 small light green leaves, 6 green-and-purple hydrangea blossoms, and 2 large light green leaves. Remove plastic stamens from hydrangea blossoms. Referring to photograph for placement, glue small leaves around hem of skirt. For collar, fold blossoms in half and glue around shoulders. For wings, glue large leaves to body as described above for the redheaded sprite.

For hanger, thread needle with a 10" length of green thread. Stitch to back of sprite at base of wings. Knot ends together to make a loop.

All Buttoned Up

If you collect decorative or antique buttons, use some of your prettiest ones to make these sparkling beauties. The ornaments get their twinkle from gleaming beads that are simply secured with straight pins.

Materials for 1 red ornament:
2 (1⅜"-diameter) pearl buttons (see note below)
scraps of felt
¼" hole punch
¾" x 9" bias strip of red velvet or velveteen
thread to match fabric
embroidery floss to match fabric
size 3 embroidery needle
16 straight pins with small white plastic heads
8 (4-mm) white pony beads
8 (3-mm) clear faceted beads

Note: If desired, use 2 (1½"-diameter) buttons and 2 smaller buttons. For each side of ornament, stack and center 1 small button on 1 large button. (For an example of this variation, see cover of book.)

Using large button as a pattern, cut 6 discs from felt. Using hole punch, make hole in center of each disc. Stack discs and whipstitch together around edges.

Referring to Diagram, cover edges of discs with strip of velvet and secure strip with running stitches. Overlap ends of strip ⅜" and trim excess velvet.

Stack 1 button (right side down), velvet-covered discs, and remaining button (right side up). Line up holes in buttons, centering holes in buttons over holes in discs. Thread needle with 6 strands of floss and sew buttons together through holes in discs.

On each of 8 pins, thread 1 faceted bead and then 1 pony bead. Referring to photograph for placement, insert pins in discs at evenly spaced intervals, alternating plain pins and pins threaded with 2 beads.

Button, Button, Who's Got the Button?

These buttoned-up ornaments prove that antique or classic buttons can give a project real distinction. That's because most new buttons don't have nearly the interest, variety, and sophistication of design found in old buttons. And as any button connoisseur will tell you, amassing a collection of beautiful vintage buttons can be fun.

If you live in a shopper's paradise like Manhattan, you may be able to begin building your collection at a specialty shop such as Tender Buttons. Located in a charming brick town house on East 62nd Street, the store carries thousands of incredible buttons—everything from exquisite antique glass buttons from Czechoslovakia to hand-polished antler buttons from Texas. (Owners Diana Epstein and Millicent Safro have opened another store in Chicago; for information on both stores, see the source listings on page 152.)

But for most button collectors, finding novel buttons involves more of a search. The best place to begin is your own attic. Locked away among the trunks of old clothes may be snazzy brass buttons from your uncle's old Navy uniform.

Thrift shops and tag sales are other promising venues. Look for old jackets, coats, and cardigans, which often have large, interesting buttons.

Antiques dealers are aware that buttons are highly collectible these days, so they keep on the lookout for good sources. Valuable items such as Venetian glass buttons are typically sold by the set. More commonly available buttons are usually massed together and sold in bulk.

Finally, if you are making a button garland or a button-covered vest—projects that call for lots and lots of buttons—and you don't want to use your best ones, take advantage of mail-order companies who sell nearly new buttons by the pound (for source listings, see page 152).

For hanger, thread needle with 6 strands of floss. Make a 1½"-long stitch through top of discs, leaving 5"-long tails of floss at beginning and end of stitch. Remove needle. Knot ends of floss together to make a loop.

Materials for 1 green ornament:
2 (1⅛"-diameter) pearl buttons
scraps of felt
¼" hole punch
¾" x 9" bias strip of green velvet or velveteen
thread to match fabric
embroidery floss to match fabric
size 3 embroidery needle
12 straight pins without small plastic heads
18 green rocaille beads
12 (3-mm) clear faceted beads
6 (5-mm) clear faceted beads

Cut and sew together felt disks and velvet strip as described for red ornament. Stack buttons and disks and sew together as described for red ornament.

On each of 6 pins, thread 1 rocaille bead and then 1 (3-mm) clear bead. On each of 6 remaining pins, thread 1 rocaille bead, 1 (3-mm) clear bead, 1

rocaille bead, and 1 (5-mm) clear bead. Referring to photograph for placement, insert pins in discs at evenly spaced intervals, alternating pins with 2 beads and pins with 4 beads.

Make hanger as described for red ornament.

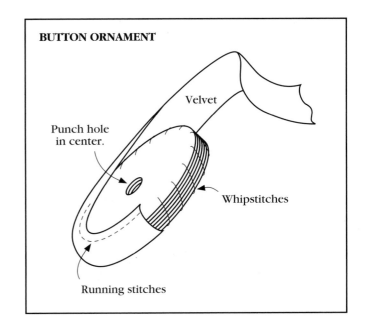

BUTTON ORNAMENT

Velvet

Punch hole in center.

Whipstitches

Running stitches

Above: To present your handmade jewelry, cover gift boxes in brown kraft paper and then line them with tissue paper. Tie dried flowers and fresh berries to the lids with yarn.

Jewelry in Gingerbread and Spongeware

This Christmas, give sweets to the sweet with Gingerbread Pins, or let someone know you think she hangs the moon with a stellar necklace. Fimo—the modeling compound we used for both sets of jewelry—simply bakes in the oven to a perfect likeness of the original designs.

Gingerbread Pins

Materials for 5 pins:
patterns on page 141
tracing paper
1 (2-ounce) package each of Fimo modeling
    compound: caramel, red
craft knife
rolling pin
round toothpick
5 pin backs
Krazy Glue or other glue that contains
    cyanoacrylate
Matte Finish Fimo Sealer (optional)

Using tracing paper, transfer patterns for desired pins and cut out.

For each shape, cut off small piece of caramel Fimo with craft knife and knead compound until pliable; roll into a small ball. Place ball on work surface and flatten with rolling pin to ⅛" thickness.

Place pattern on surface of Fimo and, using craft knife, cut out shape. Smooth edges of shape with fingertips.

Referring to pattern and photograph, form ⅜" heart or star shape from small piece of red Fimo and press firmly onto caramel shape. Referring to photograph, make a border of tiny holes just inside edges of shape with toothpick.

Bake shapes on cookie sheet in preheated oven at 250° for 20 to 30 minutes; cool completely.

If desired, apply sealer to give shapes a soft sheen. Glue pin back to back of each finished shape.

Spongeware Jewelry

Materials for Spongeware Jewelry shown:
patterns on page 142
tracing paper
1 (2-ounce) package white Fimo modeling
    compound
craft knife
rolling pin
ice pick
blue acrylic paint
sponge
2 yards of red cording, cut in half
4 pierced earring posts and backs
pin back
Krazy Glue or other glue that contains
    cyanoacrylate
Matte Finish Fimo Sealer (optional)

Moon-and-Star Jewelry: Form shapes from white Fimo as described in instructions for Gingerbread Pins. Referring to pattern, make a hole in top of each shape for necklace with ice pick.

Bake shapes on cookie sheet in preheated oven at 250° for 20 to 30 minutes; cool completely.

Dip sponge in paint and lightly dab paint onto front of shapes. Let dry. Repeat for back and edges. If desired, apply sealer to give shapes a soft sheen.

For necklace, tie knot in 1 length of cording 9" inches from end; thread cording through hole in top of small star and tie another knot, securing star between knots. Repeat to secure large star 5" from small star, and moon 3" from large star. Knot ends of cording together.

For earrings and pin, glue earring posts and pin

back to center backs of shapes. Let dry.

Heart Jewelry: Form shapes from white Fimo as described in instructions for Gingerbread Pins.

Cut a ¼" x ¾" rectangle from Fimo. Referring to Diagram, attach bottom edge of rectangle to back of heart at center top; press firmly. Fold rectangle over and attach edge to center back of heart, forming loop for cording; press end firmly.

To make beads, roll small piece of Fimo into a ½"-diameter ball. Pierce center of ball with ice pick. Form ball into cube by pressing on top, bottom, and sides of ball; remove ice pick. Repeat to make another ½" bead. Repeat, using ⅜"-diameter balls, to make 2 smaller beads.

Bake shapes on cookie sheet in preheated oven at 250° for 20 to 30 minutes; cool completely.

Dip sponge in paint and lightly dab paint onto shapes. Let dry. If desired, apply sealer to give shapes a soft sheen.

For necklace, space all shapes 1" apart, centering star on remaining length of cording and securing as described in Moon-and-Star Necklace above.

For earrings, glue earring posts to backs of shapes.

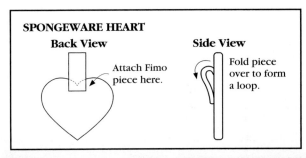

SPONGEWARE HEART
Back View — Attach Fimo piece here.
Side View — Fold piece over to form a loop.

Ideas

Gift Baskets With a Twist

Heap tokens of your affection into a basket brimming with creativity. Tailor your gifts, and your basket will be as individual as the person who receives it. Here are some snazzy presentations to inspire you.

Above: Lavish Grandmother with little luxuries. Line a white-washed wicker basket with crisp doilies and fill it with tantalizing treats: English shortbread, spiced tea, raspberry butter, potpourri, scented room freshener, fragrant soaps and cold cream, a large-print novel—and, just to pull at her heartstrings a little, a framed photo of a beloved grandchild.

Left: Delight your favorite football fanatics with a gift that will last into overtime. This Super Bowl Basket is full of epicurean goodies for the main event—hot chili seasoning, spicy nuts, gourmet mustard, imported beer, and Bloody Mary mix—all packed in air-popped popcorn.

Right: The delicacies in this authentic wok will satisfy the most discriminating palate. Oriental favorites such as Chinese mustard, plum wine, soy and duck sauces, hot-pepper sesame oil, and jasmine rice are nestled in a bed of red excelsior. Round it out with chopsticks and special cooking utensils.

Below: For those special children on your list, this activity bag bursts with fun! T-shirts with paint pens, a minigarden, cookie mix, a pasta-jewelry-making kit, and even a disposable camera for capturing the action—these are gifts that memories are made of.

Above: For those who would prefer to gather their rosebuds all day long, this "basket" is blooming with great gifts. Shears, plant markers, decorated gloves, plentiful seeds, and indispensable gardening tools fill this galvanized-metal watering can.

Instructions for the Crocheted Snowflakes and the Beaded Lace Snowflakes are on pages 59–61.

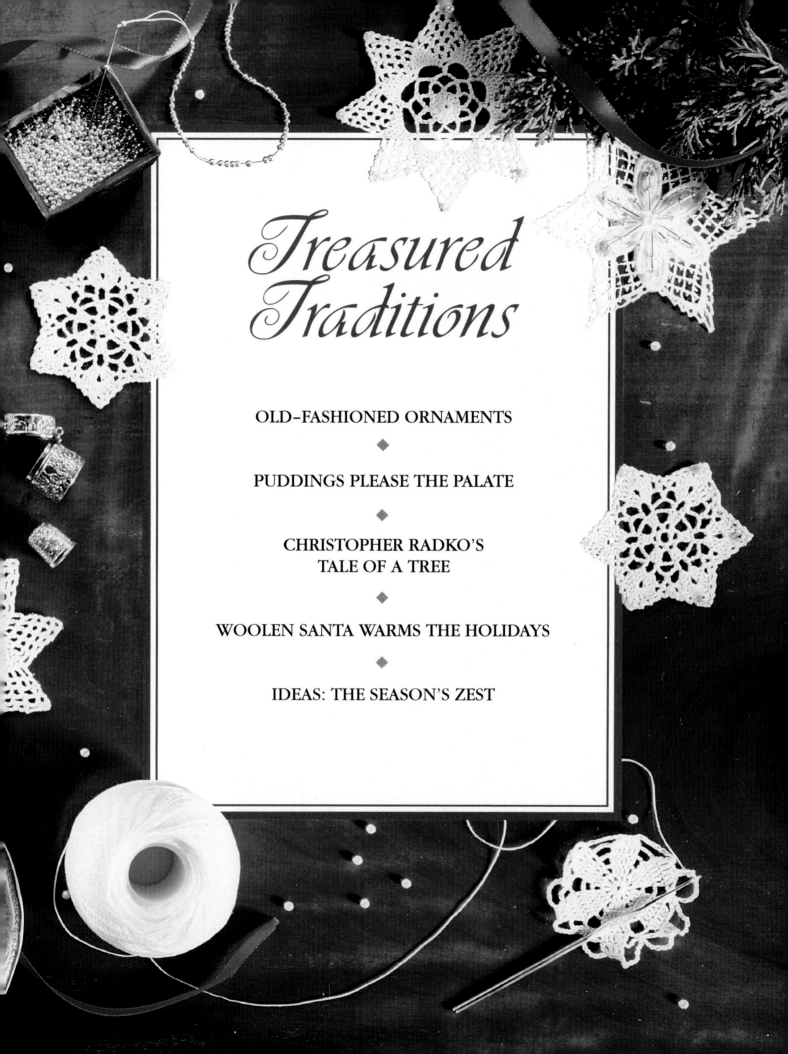

Treasured Traditions

Old-fashioned Ornaments

Until commercially manufactured ornaments became widely available in the 1870s, most Victorian families made their own. The decorations here are inspired by their creations. For some families, Crocheted Snowflakes have become a holiday tradition; learn how to start your own on page 60. Even if you don't know how to crochet, you can achieve a similar look with lacy Beaded Snowflakes on page 61.

The Victorians also fashioned paper ornaments and crafted small bunches of fabric fruit to adorn their trees. Victorian Cut-Paper Ornaments and Strawberry Clusters reprise these simple decorations of yesteryear.

Crocheted Snowflakes

Materials for 3 snowflakes:
1 (405-yard) ball of white size 20 crochet
cotton
size 10 steel crochet hook
spray starch
rustproof pins
20 (4-mm) pearl beads (optional)
beading needle (optional)
white thread (optional)
2¼ yards (⅛"-wide) red satin ribbon

Note: Crochet Abbreviations are on page 151.
SIZES: Daisy Snowflake is 4½" in diameter; Eight-Point Star Snowflake is 3¾" in diameter; Small Star Snowflake is 3" in diameter.
DAISY SNOWFLAKE: Ch 6, join with a sl st to form a ring. *Rnd 1:* Ch 4 for first dc and ch 1, (dc in ring, ch 1) 11 times, sl st in 3rd ch of beg ch-4 = 12 ch-1 sps around. *Rnd 2:* Ch 3 for first dc, (dc in ch-1 sp, dc in next dc, dc in next ch-1 sp, ch 2, dc in next dc) 5 times, dc in ch-1 sp, dc in next dc, dc in next ch-1 sp, ch 2, sl st in top of beg ch-3. *Rnd 3:* Ch 3 for first dc, dc in same st, (dc in each of next 2 dc, 2 dc

Left: Suspended from strands of red ribbon, these delicate crocheted snowflakes float gracefully inside a window. From left to right, the first three snowflakes are Daisy Snowflake, Eight-Point Star Snowflake, and Small Star Snowflake.

in next dc, ch 3, 2 dc in next dc) 5 times, dc in each of next 2 dc, 2 dc in next dc, ch 3, sl st in top of beg ch-3. *Rnd 4:* Ch 3 for first dc, dc in each of next 5 dc, * ch 4, dc in each of next 6 dc, rep from * 4 times more, ch 4, sl st in top of beg ch-3. *Rnd 5:* Ch 2, dc in next dc for first st of rnd, * dc in each of next 2 dc, keeping last lp of each st on hook, dc in each of next 2 dc, yo and pull through all lps on hook (dc-dec over 2 sts made), ch 9, dc-dec over next 2 dc, rep from * around, end last rep with ch 9, sk beg ch-2, sl st in first dc of rnd. *Rnd 6:* Ch 3 for first dc, dc in each of next 3 dc, * ch 9, sc around and over ch-lps of rnds 4 and 5, ch 9, dc in each of next 4 dc, rep from * around, end last rep with ch 9, sl st in top of beg ch-3. *Rnd 7:* Ch 2, dc in next dc for first st of rnd, dc-dec over next 2 dc, * ch 6, sc in next lp, ch 9, sc in next lp, ch 6, (dc-dec over next 2 dc) twice, rep from * around, end last rep with ch 6, sk beg ch-2, sl st in first dc of rnd. *Rnd 8:* Sl st in dc-dec and into ch-6 lp, * [(2 sc, ch 2) 3 times, 2 sc] in each ch-6 lp, [(2 sc, ch 2) 3 times, 2 sc] in ch-9 lp, ch 6, sl st in same ch-9 lp, turn, ch 1, work 8 sc in ch-6 lp just made, sl st in next sc, turn, ch 1, (sc in each of next 2 sc, ch 2) 3 times, sc in each of next 2 sc, [(2 sc, ch 2) 3 times, 2 sc] in same ch-9 lp, rep from * around as established, end with sl st in first sc of rnd. Fasten off.

FINISHING: Weave in all thread ends. Spray snowflake lightly with starch; pin to shape with rustproof pins and let dry.

If desired, before starching, sew beads to tips of snowflake with beading needle and white thread.

Cut 1 (16") length of ribbon and 1 (11") length of ribbon. Thread 16" length of ribbon through tip in snowflake; knot ends of ribbon together to make hanging loop. Tie 11" length in a bow and tack to tip of snowflake at base of hanger loop.

EIGHT-POINT STAR SNOWFLAKE: Ch 5, join with a sl st to form a ring. *Rnd 1:* Ch 3 for first dc, work 15 dc in ring, sl st in top of beg ch-3. *Rnd 2:* Ch 1, sc in same st, * ch 5, sk 1 dc, sc in next dc, rep from * 6 times more, ch 2, dc in first sc of rnd. *Rnd 3:* Ch 1, sc in lp just made, * ch 5, sc in next lp, rep from * 6 times more, ch 2, dc in first sc of rnd. *Rnd 4:* Ch 1, sc in lp just made, * ch 7, sc in next lp, rep from * 6 times more, ch 7, sl st in first sc of rnd. *Rnd 5:* Sl st into next lp, * ch 1, work 9 sc in ch-7 lp, rep from * around, end with ch 1, sl st in first sc of rnd. *Rnd 6:* Ch 1, * sc in each of next 6 sc, pull up lp in each of next 2 sc, yo and pull through all 3 lps on hook (sc-dec over 2 sts made), ch 3, sc in ch-1 sp, ch 3, sk first sc of next 9-sc group, rep from * around, end with ch 3, sl st in first sc of rnd. *Rnd 7:* Ch 1,

* sc in each of next 4 sc, sc-dec over next 2 sc, (ch 3, sc in next ch-3 lp) twice, ch 3, sk first sc of next sc-group, rep from * around, end with ch 3, sl st in first sc of rnd. *Rnd 8:* Ch 1, * sc in each of next 2 sc, sc-dec over next 2 sc, (ch 3, sc in next ch-3 lp) 3 times, ch 3, sk first sc of next sc-group, rep from * around, end with ch 3, sl st in first sc of rnd. *Rnd 9:* Ch 1, * sc-dec over next 2 sc, (ch 3, sc in next ch-3 lp) 4 times, ch 3, sk first sc of next sc-group, rep from * around, end with ch 3, sl st in first sc of rnd = 5 ch-3 lps between sc sts. Fasten off.

POINT: Join thread with sc in next ch-3 lp, (ch 3, sc in next lp) 3 times, ch 1, dc in last lp, turn, (ch 3,

---

A Flurry of Affection

Annie Laurie Spell, of Roseboro, North Carolina, has made snowflake ornaments for about 75 years. Despite her arthritis, this 88-year-old grandmother is rarely without a project at hand. Friends and family members, as well as sharp-eyed shoppers at church bazaars, welcome her intricate creations. Indeed, the ornaments have become something of a tradition for her children and grandchildren—a tradition you may want to start for your own family.

One of her granddaughters, Laurie, admired the snowflakes Annie Laurie had made over the years. So that Christmas, Annie Laurie presented Laurie and her sister, Caroline, with *50* snowflakes each! She did the same thing the next Christmas. Now covered with 100 snowflakes, Laurie's tree is a spectacular white tribute to her grandmother's love and skill.

"I have other ornaments, but all those snowflakes are so striking and delicate," says Laurie. "They're such a sentimental gift. I was overwhelmed when she gave them to me."

So that *you* won't be overwhelmed, make just a few snowflakes each year and present them to your loved ones. Before too many years go by, they will have impressive collections to enjoy for many Christmases and to hand down to the next generation.

Beaded Snowflakes: Elegant and Easy

Although these lacy ornaments resemble the crocheted versions, you don't need a crochet hook. Instead, you simply fashion each snowflake from a short length of purchased lace.

Materials for 1 snowflake:
1 length of 2½"-wide lace edging with 6 (1"-deep) points (approx. 6½" long)
white thread
powdered starch (no substitute)
1 (3") square of white felt
1 (5-mm) pearl bead
6 (½") silver bugle beads
12 (¼") silver bugle beads
18 silver seed beads

To form lace into a 6-pointed snowflake, working from right side, make 1 (½"-deep) pleat to wrong side between each point; tack in place to secure. With right sides facing, fold snowflake in half and whipstitch raw ends together to secure. Using small stitches, whipstitch snowflake at center to secure.

To flatten and stabilize snowflake, mix starch and water to make heavy starch solution, following manufacturer's instructions. Dip snowflake in starch, blot between towels, and place on ironing board. Pull points to shape snowflake and pin to secure. Using press cloth, press snowflake with hot, dry iron until dry.

Center felt on wrong side of snowflake. Using small stitches, whipstitch felt to center of snowflake, following center medallion pattern created by lace (see photograph). Trim away excess felt about ⅛" outside stitching.

Referring to photograph for placement, sew beads on right side of snowflake.

For hanger, thread 6" length of thread through 1 point and knot ends together.

---

sc in next lp) twice, ch 1, dc in last lp, turn, ch 3, sc in next lp, ch 1, dc in last lp, turn, ch 3, sl st in last lp. Fasten off. Repeat to work 7 more points on snowflake as established.

Repeat finishing steps as for Daisy Snowflake.

SMALL STAR SNOWFLAKE: Ch 6, join with a sl st to form a ring. *Rnd 1:* Ch 1, (sc in ring, ch 3) 6 times, sl st in first sc. *Rnd 2:* Sl st into next ch-3 lp, ch 3 for first dc, 2 dc in same lp, (ch 3, 3 dc in next ch-3 lp) 5 times, ch 3, sl st in top of beg ch-3. *Rnd 3:* Ch 1, sc in same st, * ch 5, sk 1 dc, sc in next dc, ch 5, sc in next dc, rep from * around, end with ch 5, sl st in first sc of rnd. *Rnd 4:* Sl st in first 2 ch of ch-5 lp, ch 3 for first dc, (2 dc, ch 2, 3 dc) in same lp, * ch 3, sc in next ch-5 lp, ch 3, (3 dc, ch 2, 3 dc) in next ch-5 lp, rep from * around, end with ch 3, sl st in top of beg ch-3. *Rnd 5:* Ch 3 for first dc, dc in each of next 2 dc, * (dc, tr, ch 1, tr, dc) in ch-2 sp, dc in each of next 3 dc, (ch 2, sc in next ch-3 lp) twice, ch 2, dc in each of next 3 dc, rep from * around, end with ch 2, sl st in top of beg ch-3. *Rnd 6:* Sl st in next dc, ch 1, sc in same st, * ch 2, sk 1 dc, sc in next dc, ch 2, (sc, ch 2, sc) in ch-1 sp, ch 2, sk tr, sc in next dc, ch 2, sk 1 dc, sc in next dc, sk 1 dc, (ch 2, sc in next ch-2 sp) 3 times, ch 2, sk 1 dc, sc in next dc, rep from * around, end with ch 2, sl st in first sc. Fasten off.

Repeat finishing steps as for Daisy Snowflake.

Victorian Cut-Paper Ornaments

Materials for 1 boot or shoe:
patterns on pages 144–45
tracing paper
1 (8½" x 11") sheet of medium-weight
   cardboard
1 (8½" x 11") sheet of embossed foil paper:
   gold (for Gold Boot) or silver (for Black
   Boot)
1 (8½" x 11") sheet of glazed wrapping paper:
   red (for Gold Boot) or black (for Flower
   Shoe or Black Boot)
rubber cement
6"-diameter white paper doily (for Gold Boot)
20" length of gold paper or fabric lace (for
   Flower Shoe)
4 small flower "scrap" pictures (for Flower
   Shoe; see source listing on page 152)
6" length of gold braid

Note: Other traditional shapes include lyres, bug-
gies, and stars. The ornaments can also be trimmed
with foil stars, greeting-card pictures, tinsel, chenille, scraps of cording, or rickrack.

Using tracing paper, transfer desired shoe or boot
pattern to cardboard and cut out for base. For Gold
Boot, transfer pattern to gold foil and cut out; also
transfer trim patterns to red glazed paper and cut
out. For Flower Shoe or Black Boot, transfer pattern
to black glazed paper and cut out. For Black Boot,
also transfer trim patterns to silver foil and cut out.

Using rubber cement, glue foil or paper boot or
shoe piece to cardboard base, aligning edges. Referring to pattern for placement, glue trim to boot or
shoe piece. For Gold Boot, fold doily in half. Shape
doily so ruffled edge matches shape of boot top.
Glue to wrong side of boot so ruffled edge extends
above top of boot. Glue tulip trim to wrong side of
boot so tips show just above ruffle.

Referring to pattern for placement, trim Flower
Shoe with pieces of lace. Glue flower pictures to
shoe (see photograph).

To make hanging loop, fold gold braid in half and
glue ends to back of ornament.

*Right: Hang these rich velveteen strawberries on your
Victorian-style tree, or pin a cluster to a hat and
enjoy their appealing texture all year long.*

*Below: Although the Victorians hung them on trees, these
cut-paper ornaments also make an unusual garland.*

Strawberry Clusters

Materials for 1 cluster:
patterns on page 142
tracing paper
scraps of red velveteen
3 (2½") velvet florist's leaves
thread to match fabric
polyester stuffing
1 skein each of size 8 pearl cotton or
**   embroidery floss: red, green**
size 8 embroidery needle
craft glue

Note: Patterns include ⅛" seam allowances. If using embroidery floss, use 3 strands as 1 length.

Using tracing paper, transfer 1 large strawberry and 2 small strawberry patterns to red velveteen and cut out. Transfer 3 large leaf and 6 small leaf patterns to florist's leaves and cut out.

With right sides facing and raw edges aligned, fold large strawberry piece in half lengthwise and stitch side seam from small dot to large dot. Turn and stuff firmly. Run a gathering thread around top raw edge by hand. Pull to gather, closing opening. Secure thread. Repeat for 2 small strawberries.

Using 1 length of red pearl cotton, embroider surface of each strawberry with evenly spaced French knots. (See diagram for French knot on page 70.)

Cut 6 (7") lengths of green pearl cotton. Holding lengths together as 1, tie knot at 1 end. Pin knot to work surface and separate lengths into 3 even groups. Referring to Diagram below, braid lengths for 2¾" and tie knot at end of braiding. Braid 3 lengths for 2¼" and knot. Braid remaining 3 lengths for 1½" and knot. Trim excess strands close to knots.

Referring to Diagram, sew knot at top of braid to top of large strawberry. Sew bottom 2 knots to tops of small strawberries.

Referring to photograph, glue 3 large leaves to top of large strawberry and 3 small leaves to top of each small strawberry.

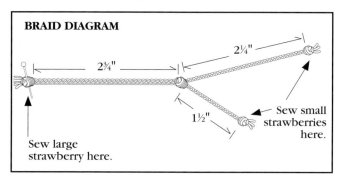

BRAID DIAGRAM

2¾"

2¼"

1½"

Sew large
strawberry here.

Sew small
strawberries
here.

Above: Orange-Pecan Plum Pudding topped with Citrus Hard Sauce is a scrumptious variation on traditional plum pudding, the highlight of an English Christmas dinner. For more on this time-honored dessert, see the box on the opposite page.

Puddings Please the Palate

In Britain, puddings are more than creamy desserts. Some are dense and spongy, while others are thick and custardy. The holiday treats featured here are just as diverse, but they have one thing in common: They are every bit as tempting as their old-world counterparts.

Orange-Pecan Plum Pudding

½ cup butter or margarine, softened
¾ cup sugar
3 large eggs
¾ teaspoon grated orange rind
2½ cups all-purpose flour, divided
1 teaspoon baking soda
1 teaspoon ground cinnamon
¼ teaspoon ground allspice
Dash of ground cloves
¼ cup milk
¼ cup frozen orange juice concentrate, thawed
1 small cooking apple, peeled, cored, and grated
1 cup chopped pecans
1 cup semisweet chocolate minimorsels
3 tablespoons minced crystallized gingerroot
Citrus Hard Sauce (recipe follows)

Note: For information on ordering a steamed pudding mold, see source listing on page 152.

Beat butter at medium-high speed of an electric mixer until creamy; gradually add sugar, beating well.

Add eggs, 1 at a time, beating well after each addition. Stir in orange rind.

Combine 2 cups flour and next 4 ingredients. Add dry ingredients to creamed mixture alternately with milk and orange juice concentrate, beginning and ending with flour mixture. Mix well after each addition.

Toss apple, pecans, chocolate morsels, and gingerroot with reserved ½ cup flour; fold into batter. Spoon batter into a well-greased 6-cup pudding mold; cover tightly.

Place mold on shallow rack in a large, deep kettle with enough boiling water to come halfway up mold. Cover kettle; steam pudding 3 hours in continuously boiling water (replace water as needed). Remove mold from water and cool 10 minutes. Loosen pudding from sides of mold and unmold onto a serving platter. Serve with Citrus Hard Sauce. Yield: 8 servings.

Citrus Hard Sauce

½ cup butter or margarine, softened
1½ cups sifted powdered sugar
1½ tablespoons Grand Marnier or other orange-flavored liqueur

Beat butter and sugar at medium-high speed of an electric mixer until smooth. Gradually add Grand Marnier, beating until blended. Cover and chill. Yield: 1 cup.

Note: A hard sauce, when served over a warm dessert, slowly melts.

A Simply Plummy Pudding

Despite the fact that the recipe contains not a single plum, plum pudding has a venerable history.

The dessert dates from the Middle Ages, and during the Puritan reign in England it was even outlawed as "sinfully rich."

In Victorian times, each family member took a turn stirring the batter while making a wish. Then a sixpence was stirred into the batter; whoever found it on Christmas Day was guaranteed good luck in the coming year.

With Orange-Pecan Plum Pudding, you could make these rituals part of your family's holiday traditions—just be sure to wrap your coin in aluminum foil before folding it into the batter.

Vanilla Rice Pudding

1 vanilla bean
6 cups milk
1 cup medium-grain rice, uncooked
½ cup sugar
¼ teaspoon salt
⅓ cup firmly packed brown sugar
⅛ teaspoon ground cinnamon
1 tablespoon butter or margarine

Split vanilla bean in half lengthwise; scrape vanilla seeds from bean into a medium saucepan. Add milk and next 3 ingredients; stir well. Bring mixture to a boil. Reduce heat and simmer, uncovered, stirring frequently, 35 minutes or until mixture is thick. Cover and chill thoroughly. Discard bean halves.

Spoon pudding into a lightly greased 2-quart baking dish. Combine brown sugar and cinnamon; sprinkle evenly over top of pudding. Dot with butter. Broil 5½" from heat 2 to 3 minutes or until sugar and butter melt. Yield: 8 to 10 servings.

Drenched Gingerbread Pudding

½ cup butter or margarine, softened
¼ cup firmly packed brown sugar
1 large egg
⅔ cup molasses
2⅓ cups all-purpose flour
1½ teaspoons baking soda
½ teaspoon salt
1½ teaspoons ground ginger
¾ teaspoon ground cinnamon
¼ teaspoon ground cloves
1 cup hot water
1 cup sifted powdered sugar
½ teaspoon grated lemon rind
¼ cup fresh lemon juice
Garnish: sweetened whipped cream,
　　lemon peel

Beat butter at medium-high speed of an electric mixer until creamy; gradually add brown sugar, beating well.

Add egg and molasses, beating well.

Combine flour and next 5 ingredients; add to creamed mixture alternately with hot water, beginning and ending with flour mixture. Mix after each addition.

Pour batter into a greased and floured 9"-square pan. Bake at 350° for 30 to 35 minutes or until a wooden pick inserted in center comes out clean.

Combine powdered sugar, lemon rind, and lemon juice in a small saucepan; stir well. Bring mixture to a boil; boil 1 minute and remove from heat.

Using a wooden pick, poke holes in top of gingerbread pudding. Slowly pour syrup mixture over pudding. Cool 15 minutes. Garnish, if desired. Yield: 9 servings.

Buttermilk Pear Pudding with Caramel Sauce

⅓ cup butter or margarine, softened
1 cup sugar, divided
2 large eggs
1¼ cups all-purpose flour
1 teaspoon ground cinnamon, divided
¼ teaspoon ground allspice
¼ teaspoon ground nutmeg
½ teaspoon baking soda
½ cup buttermilk
⅓ cup pear preserves
⅓ cup all-purpose flour
¼ cup butter or margarine, softened
Caramel Sauce (recipe follows)

Beat ⅓ cup butter at medium speed of an electric mixer until creamy; gradually add ½ cup sugar, beating well. Add eggs, 1 at a time, beating well after each addition. Combine 1¼ cups flour, ½ teaspoon cinnamon, and next 2 ingredients; stir well and set aside. Dissolve baking soda in buttermilk. Add flour mixture to creamed mixture alternately with buttermilk mixture, beginning and ending with flour mixture. Stir in pear preserves.

Pour batter into a greased and floured 9"-square pan. Combine remaining ½ cup sugar, ⅓ cup flour, and remaining ½ teaspoon cinnamon; cut in ¼ cup butter with pastry blender until mixture is crumbly. Sprinkle over batter. Bake at 350° for 25 minutes or until a wooden pick inserted in center comes out clean. Cool completely in pan before cutting. Serve with Caramel Sauce. Yield: 9 servings.

Caramel Sauce

½ cup sugar
¼ cup butter
½ cup whipping cream
¾ cup chopped pecans, toasted (optional)

Sprinkle sugar into a small cast-iron skillet. Cook over medium heat, stirring constantly with a wooden spoon, until sugar melts and turns light brown. Remove from heat; add butter and stir until blended.

Left: Star-shaped lemon garnish adds sparkle to Drenched Gingerbread Pudding. To make the shapes, peel a lemon and lay the peel flat. Cut out the star shapes with tiny aspic cutters (see the source listing on page 152).

Return mixture to low heat; gradually add whipping cream to hot mixture, 2 tablespoons at a time, stirring constantly. Continue to cook mixture over low heat, stirring constantly, 10 minutes or until mixture is thickened and creamy. If desired, stir in pecans. Serve warm over Buttermilk Pear Pudding. Yield: 1 cup.

French Bread Pudding with Apple-Bourbon Sauce

1 (1-pound) loaf French bread
¾ cup raisins
1 (2-ounce) package slivered almonds, toasted and chopped
4 large eggs
1 cup sugar
3 tablespoons butter or margarine, melted
1½ teaspoons vanilla extract
2¼ cups milk
1¼ cups half-and-half
¾ cup bourbon
Apple-Bourbon Sauce (recipe follows)

Cut off and discard crusty ends of bread. Tear rest of loaf into bite-size chunks. Arrange in a heavily greased 13" x 9" x 2" baking dish. Sprinkle raisins and almonds over bread. Set aside. Beat eggs in a large bowl until thick and pale; add sugar, butter, and vanilla, beating until blended. Gradually add milk, half-and-half, and bourbon, beating well. Pour egg mixture over bread. Cover and chill 8 hours.

Bake, uncovered, at 350° for 45 minutes or until lightly browned and set. Cool about 20 minutes before cutting into squares. Serve with Apple-Bourbon Sauce. Yield: 12 servings.

Apple-Bourbon Sauce

½ cup butter or margarine
1 cup firmly packed brown sugar
½ cup bourbon
½ teaspoon ground cinnamon
3 medium-size Rome apples, cored and thinly sliced

Melt butter in a large skillet over medium-low heat; stir in brown sugar, bourbon, and cinnamon. Cook until sugar melts.

Add apple; cook, stirring frequently, until apples are glazed and crisp-tender. Yield: 2 cups.

Christopher Radko's Tale of a Tree

*For ornament designer Christopher Radko, Christmas 1984 was grim.
But from the loss of his family heirlooms came a tradition renewed.*

When Christopher was growing up in Scarsdale, New York, the highlight of his family's Christmas was decorating the tree with their astonishing collection of blown-glass ornaments. Three generations of Radkos had collected more than 2,000 of the handcrafted beauties; as a boy, Christopher loved to slide under the tree's lowest branches and look up at all the shimmering spheres.

In 1984, the holidays were unfolding as usual. Christopher was removing sap and needles from the old tree stand—the annual chore that always fell to him—when he decided that a new one was in order. After a bit of shopping around, he bought a stand guaranteed to hold a tree up to 18 feet in height, a good 4 feet taller than the Radkos' own tree, and the fun of decorating the tree went on as always.

One cold December morning, though, the worst happened. Despite its guarantee, the stand buckled and the tree crashed to the floor, shattering more than half of the fragile decorations.

"I was absolutely heartbroken," Christopher remembers. "Even though I knew there was no way I could replace the ornaments my great-grandmother and grandmother had handed down, I thought that the least I could do was buy some substitutes so our tree wouldn't look so forlorn." He searched stores in Scarsdale, and he shopped in New York City. When he finally discovered figural glass ornaments were no longer being made, he thought, sadly, that was that.

The next spring, while Christopher was visiting relatives in Poland, a cousin introduced him to a farmer who once made blown-glass ornaments; he might be able to make a few new ones. There was only one catch: Christopher had to supply him with detailed drawings of exactly what kinds of ornaments he wanted. Upon seeing the designs, the glassblower said that they were just like the ornaments his father and grandfather had made before World War II; although he'd never made such complicated pieces before, he would be happy to try.

After Christopher returned to the States with his newly crafted glass ornaments, family members and friends clamored for reproductions of their own. He realized then he had discovered not just a need but his own knack for filling it.

Today, only eight years later, Christopher busies teams of Polish, German, Czechoslovakian, and Italian glassblowers with limited editions of his ornaments—the 1993 line features over 400 dazzling designs. Ideas come not only from memories of his family's antique ornaments but from Christopher's other inspirations—

Left: These days Christopher is surrounded by ornaments like those he loved as a child. Clockwise from top left, here is just a sprinkling from Christopher's 1993 line: Jingle Bells Garland, Nautilus Shell, Jumbo Spintop, Harlequin, and the whimsical Santa Tree.

architecture, fabrics, films, and museum collections. It takes about a week to make each ornament, which is blown, silvered, lacquered, painted, and glittered entirely by hand. Among Christopher's most unusual ornaments are his figural ones—his latest lines have featured a pipe-smoking monkey, a cowboy Santa, and even a Fu Manchu.

"My company's success has allowed me to revive Christmas crafts and techniques that were all but lost," Christopher explains. "With my annual collection of new designs, I am reviving a tradition of designing that had its heyday at the turn of the century. My glassblowers are resurrecting old molds and relearning skills that their cottage industry hasn't used in 70 years. Now even young apprentice glassblowers are being trained in the traditions of their great-grandfathers, ensuring that fine glass ornaments will continue being made well into the next century. That's something to celebrate."

Because about half of the ornaments in the line are retired or changed in some way each year, Christopher's ornaments are highly collectible. Katharine Hepburn, Bruce Springsteen, Dolly Parton, and Hillary Rodham Clinton are all devoted collectors. There's even a Radko ornament club and quarterly newsletter. (For information on both the collectors' club and Radko ornaments, see the source listings on pages 152–53.)

But perhaps the most wonderful thing about Christopher's success is that now any of us can decorate our tree with exquisitely old-fashioned blown-glass ornaments. And thanks to Christopher, we don't have to travel to Europe to find them.

"The World's Best Tree Stand"

"After the tragic tree crash of 1984," says Christopher, "I searched out what may be *the* finest tree stand available. It's solidly crafted and extremely heavy—there's no way my tree can budge by even an inch." Made of cast iron, the stand also has a black enamel finish to guard against rusting. Another plus: It's made in America. For a source listing, see page 153.

Woolen Santa Warms the Holidays

With his jaunty hat and long beard, this dear Santa smiles serenely between the branches of a Christmas tree. His kindly visage possesses a sculpted nose, simple embroidery, and a blithe spirit.

Materials:
patterns on page 143
tracing paper
⅛ yard of cream wool fabric
⅛ yard of burgundy wool fabric
3" square of rosy beige wool fabric
dressmaker's pen
thread: cream, beige
embroidery floss: black, dark green,
**   burgundy, cream**
size 8 embroidery needle
polyester stuffing
pencil with eraser
cosmetic powder blush

Note: Patterns include ¼" seam allowances, unless otherwise noted. Press wool with a steam iron to shrink before marking or cutting.

Using tracing paper, transfer patterns to fabrics and cut out. Mark center notches with ⅛" cuts into seam allowances.

For head front, using dressmaker's pen, mark face outline on 1 head piece. To remove face, make a small horizontal slit in center of face area and trim, leaving ⅛" seam allowance. Clip curves about ⅛" apart in seam allowance.

Center head front over beige face square; pin or baste together. Starting from back of face and using a doubled strand of cream sewing thread, reverse-appliqué beige face to head front, using needle's point to turn ⅛" seam allowance under as you sew. Trim beige wool ¼" from seam.

Using dressmaker's pen, transfer facial features and holly to head front. Using 3 strands of floss and embroidery needle, embroider facial features and holly. (See Embroidery Diagrams and pattern.)

With right sides facing, raw edges aligned, and notches matching, stitch 1 hat piece to 1 head piece. Clip curves along top of head piece and bottom of hat piece. Repeat for remaining hat and head pieces. Press seams toward hat.

With right sides facing and raw edges aligned, stitch front to back, leaving open where indicated on pattern. Clip curves and turn.

Stuff firmly, using eraser of pencil to stuff points. Slipstitch opening closed.

Using a doubled strand of beige sewing thread, sculpt nose as follows: Working point of needle between wool threads on 1 side of face along seam, make an opening big enough for knotted end of thread. Push needle ¼" down into stuffing and bring needle up at bottom of 1 nose line, burying knot in stuffing. Use point of needle to realign wool threads.

Make tiny stitches back and forth between 2 nose lines, dipping needle into stuffing and pulling thread slightly to define nose. Referring to photograph, continue stitching to top of nose. To secure thread, pull needle through stuffing to bottom back seam of hat, and backstitch. Trim thread close to fabric.

Apply blush to cheeks with pencil eraser. Stitch 3 (6") strands of burgundy floss through top of hat and knot ends together to make hanging loop.

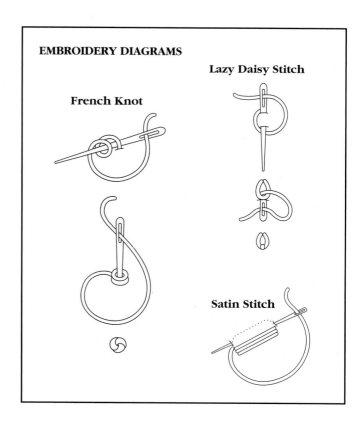

EMBROIDERY DIAGRAMS

French Knot

Lazy Daisy Stitch

Satin Stitch

The Season's Zest

Crystalline cartwheels of dried citrus are rich in texture and jewel-like in color. Indeed, these decorations of grapefruit, orange, lemon, and lime add a slice of the season any way you cut them!

Generations of Americans regard citrus as a special Christmas treat—a bit of sunshine in the heart of winter. These glistening rounds of dried citrus capitalize on that warm sentiment and allow you to create some sunny designs of your own.

The fruit shown on these pages was dried in a food dehydrator, which is now the method of choice for successful drying. Dehydrators are widely available in large department and specialty stores. Fruit dried in a dehydrator retains more of its true color than fruit dried by other means. While using the dehydrator is the easiest method we've tried, you can also dry fruit using the traditional method in a low-heat oven.

To dry citrus fruit in a dehydrator: Cut unpeeled fruit into ⅛– to ¼–inch slices. Following manufacturer's directions, place slices ½ inch apart on the dehydrator racks. Allow to aerate for 4 to 12 hours* or until slices are dry to the touch.

To dry citrus fruit in the oven: Place sliced fruit on a wire rack on top of a cookie sheet and place in a 200-degree oven. Leave in oven for 6 to 10 hours* or until fruit is leathery. Remove fruit from oven and let air-dry on rack until fruit is dry to the touch.

Note: Drying time will vary with the type of fruit, the thicknesses of the slices, the humidity, and the method of dehydration used.

Left: A gift badge that will serve later as an ornament adds a thoughtful touch to your packages. Hot-glue dried bay leaves and a whole clove to the top of a dehydrated grapefruit slice; finish with a twist of red ribbon for a hanger. Use the same method to create the orange-slice ornaments on the opposite page.

Above: For a luminous table display, pair orange slices with floating candles in an amber glow of apple juice. The lush wreath of orange slices, cinnamon sticks, and tallow berries was created by Joy Jowell of Seabrook, Texas (for more on Joy's splendid wreaths, see pages 6–7). Be advised—this looks so delicious that guests may be tempted to drink it; let them know it is just for display!

Above: Dressed for the holidays in a citrus cloak, this radiant topiary tree is a stylish arrangement for a mantel or sideboard. To construct it, use hot-glue to cover a 15-inch-tall Styrofoam cone with moss and then glue dehydrated orange, lemon, and lime slices in rows around the tree. For design interest, intermix slices that have been cut in half. Insert a stick into the base of the tree and secure the topiary in a florist's-foam base placed in a decorative pot. Fill in around the base with cuttings of ivy and boxwood.

The recipe for the Noah's Ark Cookies is on pages 86-87;
instructions for the stenciled napkins are on page 149.

A Country Christmas Pantry

Above: A crock of Pepper-Corn Chowder and either Touch-of-Wheat Onion Bread (left) or Cheddar Scones (right) make a flavorful meal without fuss. For a quick holiday look, use raffia to tie berries and greenery to brass candlesticks.

Homemade Soups and Hearty Breads

After a cold day of holiday shopping, nothing warms you like home-cooked soup and crusty bread. Make these convenient recipes early and reheat them when you get back. Their aromas will entice you to take a break from hectic preparations and enjoy a simple and satisfying meal.

Pepper-Corn Chowder

6 slices bacon
1 medium onion, chopped
2 stalks celery, thinly sliced
1 teaspoon minced jalapeño pepper
2 medium red potatoes, peeled and cubed
2 cups frozen whole kernel corn, thawed
2 cups half-and-half
1 cup milk
1 ($8^3/_4$-ounce) can cream-style corn
1 teaspoon beef-flavored bouillon granules
$^3/_4$ teaspoon salt
$^1/_4$ teaspoon sugar
1 bay leaf, crumbled
1 cup chopped sweet red pepper
2 teaspoons butter or margarine, melted

Cook bacon in a large skillet until crisp; remove bacon, reserving drippings in skillet. Crumble bacon and set aside. Sauté onion, celery, and jalapeño pepper in drippings, stirring constantly, until tender.

Transfer sautéed vegetables to a large saucepan; add potato and next 8 ingredients. Bring to a boil; reduce heat and simmer, uncovered, 25 to 30 minutes or until potato is tender.

Sauté red pepper in butter in a small skillet over medium heat until tender. Stir into soup before serving. To serve, ladle soup into individual bowls and top with crumbled bacon. Yield: 7½ cups.

Oven-Baked Beef Ragout

3 tablespoons all-purpose flour
½ teaspoon salt
½ teaspoon pepper
2 pounds beef stew meat, cut into 1" pieces
3 tablespoons olive oil, divided
4 small sweet potatoes, peeled and cut into 2" pieces
2 medium onions, cut into 2" pieces
18 pitted prunes, halved
2½ cups sweet red wine
2 cups water
1½ teaspoons beef-flavored bouillon granules
½ teaspoon dried rosemary, crushed
½ teaspoon salt
¼ teaspoon pepper

Combine first 3 ingredients in a large zip-top plastic bag; add stew meat. Seal bag and shake to coat meat thoroughly.

Brown half of beef in 1½ tablespoons olive oil in a large oven-proof Dutch oven over medium-high heat. Remove browned beef to a platter with a slotted spoon; set aside and keep warm. Repeat procedure with remaining beef and 1½ tablespoons oil. Discard drippings.

Return reserved beef to Dutch oven. Add sweet potato and remaining ingredients; stir well. Cover and bake at 325° for 1 hour and 40 minutes; uncover and bake an additional 50 minutes or until meat is very tender. To serve, ladle soup into individual serving bowls. Yield: 10 cups.

Italian Vegetable Soup

2 medium leeks
3 medium carrots, cut into julienne strips
2 tablespoons olive oil
2 medium zucchini, sliced
1 (28-ounce) can whole tomatoes, undrained and chopped
1 (15-ounce) can dark red kidney beans, drained
2 (14½-ounce) cans ready-to-serve chicken broth
1 teaspoon dried Italian seasoning
½ teaspoon salt
¼ teaspoon garlic powder
¼ teaspoon pepper
4 ounces Christmas tree-shaped pasta (see source listing on page 153) or macaroni
⅓ cup grated Parmesan cheese
¼ cup chopped fresh parsley
Garlic Croutons (recipe follows)

Remove roots, tough outer leaves, and tops from leeks, leaving 4" of dark leaves. Split leeks in half lengthwise; wash well. Slice leeks thinly and set aside.

Sauté carrot in hot oil in a Dutch oven until tender-crisp. Add leeks and sauté 5 to 8 minutes or until vegetables are tender. Stir in zucchini and next 7 ingredients; stir well. Bring mixture to a boil; add pasta. Reduce heat and simmer 10 to 12 minutes or until pasta is tender. Stir in Parmesan cheese and parsley. To serve, ladle soup into individual soup bowls and top with Garlic Croutons. Yield: 10 cups.

Garlic Croutons

½ (1-pound) loaf Italian bread
2 tablespoons butter or margarine, softened
½ teaspoon garlic powder

Slice bread into ½"-thick slices. Spread softened butter over 1 side of each bread slice; sprinkle with garlic powder. Cut slices into ½" cubes. Place on a baking sheet and bake at 375° for 15 minutes or until crisp and dry. Yield: 4 cups.

Spinach-and-Tomato Soup

1 large onion, thinly sliced and separated into
  rings
3 tablespoons butter or margarine, melted
3 cups chicken broth, divided
2 cups half-and-half
3 tablespoons all-purpose flour
1 (10-ounce) package fresh spinach, chopped
3 medium tomatoes, peeled, seeded, and
  chopped
½ teaspoon salt
¼ teaspoon pepper
¼ teaspoon dried dillweed
3 hard-cooked eggs, grated or finely chopped

Sauté onion in butter in a large Dutch oven until
tender. Stir in 2½ cups chicken broth and half-and-
half. Bring just to a simmer; simmer 10 minutes.
Combine remaining ½ cup chicken broth and flour,
stirring until smooth. Add to Dutch oven; stir well.
Cook over medium heat, stirring constantly, until
mixture is slightly thickened.

Stir in spinach and next 4 ingredients. Cook 5
minutes or until spinach wilts and soup is thoroughly heated. To serve, ladle soup into individual bowls
and top with grated egg. Yield: 9 cups.

Pecan Corn Muffins

⅔ cup finely chopped pecans
3 tablespoons maple syrup
1⅓ cups all-purpose flour
1 cup yellow cornmeal
1 tablespoon sugar
2½ teaspoons baking powder
½ teaspoon baking soda
½ teaspoon salt
1¼ cups buttermilk
⅓ cup butter or margarine, melted
1 large egg, beaten
1 egg yolk

Combine pecans and maple syrup; stir well and
set aside.

Combine flour and next 5 ingredients in a large
bowl; make a well in center of flour mixture.

Combine buttermilk, melted butter, egg, and egg
yolk; stir well. Add to flour mixture, stirring just until moistened. Spoon about 2 tablespoons batter into
greased muffin pans. Spoon about 1 tablespoon
reserved pecan mixture over batter. Top pecan

mixture with remaining batter. Bake at 375° for 25
to 27 minutes or until lightly browned. Remove
from pans immediately. Cool 10 minutes before serving. Yield: about 1 dozen.

Cheddar Scones

2 cups all-purpose flour
2 teaspoons baking powder
½ teaspoon salt
½ teaspoon dried thyme
¼ teaspoon ground red pepper
¼ cup plus 2 tablespoons butter or margarine
½ cup (2 ounces) shredded sharp Cheddar
  cheese
⅔ cup buttermilk
2 teaspoons Dijon mustard
1 tablespoon butter or margarine, melted
Sesame seeds or poppy seeds

Combine first 5 ingredients in a large bowl; stir
well. Cut in butter with a pastry blender until mixture is crumbly. Stir in cheese. Combine buttermilk
and mustard; stir well and add to flour mixture, stirring just until dry ingredients are moistened.

Turn dough out onto a lightly floured surface and
knead lightly 4 or 5 times. Pat dough into a 7" circle
on a greased baking sheet. Using a sharp knife, cut
circle into 8 wedges; separate wedges slightly. Brush
tops of wedges with melted butter; sprinkle with
sesame seeds or poppy seeds. Bake at 425° for 15
minutes or until golden. Serve warm. Yield: 8
scones.

Touch-of-Wheat Onion Bread

5 cups all-purpose flour
¾ cup whole wheat flour
2 tablespoons dried minced onion
1 tablespoon salt
¼ teaspoon pepper
2 packages dry yeast
1 tablespoon sugar
1 cup warm water (105° to 115°)
1 cup milk
3 tablespoons vegetable oil
2 tablespoons spicy brown mustard
1 large egg, lightly beaten
1 egg white, lightly beaten
1 tablespoon dried minced onion
1 tablespoon water

Combine first 5 ingredients; stir well and set aside.

Dissolve yeast and sugar in warm water in a large bowl; let stand 5 minutes. Add milk and next 3 ingredients; stir well. Gradually stir in enough flour mixture to make a stiff dough.

Turn dough out onto a floured surface and knead 4 or 5 times. Shape dough into a ball. Place dough in a well-greased bowl, turning to grease top. Cover and let rise in a warm place (85°), free from drafts, 1 hour or until doubled in bulk.

Punch dough down; let rest 5 minutes. Divide dough in half. Shape each half into a round loaf; place on 2 greased baking sheets. Let rise in a warm place, free from drafts, 20 minutes or until doubled in bulk.

Combine egg white, dried minced onion, and water; stir well and brush on loaves. Bake at 375° for 30 minutes or until loaves sound hollow when tapped. Cool slightly before slicing. Yield: 2 loaves.

Parmesan Flatbread

1 package dry yeast
1¼ cups warm water (105° to 115°)
5 to 5½ cups bread flour, divided
2 tablespoons grated Parmesan cheese
1 tablespoon sugar
2 teaspoons salt
¾ cup beer, at room temperature
2 tablespoons olive oil
3 tablespoons yellow cornmeal
Olive oil
½ cup freshly grated Parmesan cheese
2 teaspoons coarse salt

Dissolve yeast in warm water; let stand 5 minutes.

Combine 1 cup flour and next 3 ingredients in a large bowl. Add yeast mixture, beer, and 2 tablespoons olive oil; stir well. Cover and let stand in a warm place (85°), free from drafts, 30 minutes or until dough is very bubbly.

Gradually stir in enough of the remaining flour to make a soft dough. Turn dough out onto a heavily floured surface and knead until smooth and elastic (about 8 to 10 minutes). Let dough rest 10 minutes.

Sprinkle 2 (14") pizza pans evenly with cornmeal; set aside. Divide dough into 2 equal portions. Roll 1 portion of dough into a 14" circle and place on prepared pizza pan; press to edges. Repeat procedure with remaining dough. Prick dough several times with a fork. Brush each circle generously with olive

oil and sprinkle evenly with freshly grated Parmesan cheese and coarse salt. Cover and let rise in a warm place, free from drafts, 20 minutes. Bake at 425° for 15 minutes or until golden. Serve warm. Yield: 2 loaves.

Below: Pair Italian Vegetable Soup with Parmesan Flatbread in a heartwarming gift basket. Christmas ornaments such as these apples will remind recipients of your gift throughout the holidays. We added extra bags of the Christmas tree-shaped pasta used in the soup (see the source listing on page 153). For more gift-basket ideas, see pages 54-55.

Salsas and Spreads: Gifts That Taste Good

Flavorful and festive, these easy-to-make concoctions are wonderful to keep on hand to serve drop-in company. That means they make terrific gifts, too, for the hosts and hostesses on your list.

Oriental Pineapple-Mustard Sauce

⅔ cup pineapple preserves
⅓ cup prepared mustard
1 tablespoon teriyaki sauce
1 teaspoon peeled and grated gingerroot

Combine all ingredients in a small bowl; stir well. Store in glass containers in refrigerator. Serve warm, chilled, or at room temperature with ham, chicken, egg rolls, or shrimp. Yield: 1 cup.

Sherry-Apricot Mustard

½ cup cream sherry
⅓ cup honey
¼ cup lemon juice
1 (6-ounce) package dried apricots
1 cup Dijon mustard

Combine first 4 ingredients in a medium saucepan; stir well. Bring to a boil and cook, stirring constantly, until honey melts. Cover; reduce heat and simmer 15 minutes. Uncover and simmer an additional 15 minutes, stirring occasionally. Remove from heat; cool.

Position knife blade in food processor bowl; transfer apricot mixture to food processor bowl. Process until smooth. Transfer mixture to a medium bowl; stir in Dijon mustard. Store in glass containers in refrigerator. Serve with ham or pork. Yield: 2 cups.

Left: Ready for gifting, salsas and spreads capitalize on the trend toward flavor-packed condiments. Clockwise from bottom: Pineapple Salsa, Remoulade Sauce, Orange Mustard, Cranberry-Kumquat Salsa, and Vegetable-Olive Salsa.

Cajun Onion Mustard

1 cup minced onion
¾ cup minced sweet red pepper
¼ cup sugar
½ teaspoon dried crushed red pepper
1 cup prepared mustard

Combine first 4 ingredients in a medium saucepan. Cook, stirring constantly, over medium heat until sugar dissolves. Cook, stirring frequently, an additional 20 minutes or until liquid is evaporated. Remove from heat and cool. Stir in mustard. Store in glass containers in refrigerator. Serve with hamburgers, hot dogs, or ham, or use as a sandwich spread. Yield: 1½ cups.

Orange Mustard

1 (6-ounce) can frozen orange juice concentrate, thawed and undiluted
¼ cup honey
¼ cup white wine vinegar
1 cup coarse-grained mustard
2 tablespoons grated orange rind
3 egg yolks

Combine first 3 ingredients in a small saucepan; bring to a boil and cook, stirring constantly, until honey melts. Boil, uncovered, over medium heat 40 minutes or until mixture is reduced to ¾ cup, stirring occasionally to prevent sticking. (Do not boil over high heat; mixture will burn.)

Combine last 3 ingredients; stir well. Stir one-third of reduced mixture into mustard mixture; add mustard mixture to remaining reduced mixture, stirring well. Cook, stirring constantly, over medium-low heat until mixture thickens. Cool. Store in glass containers in refrigerator. Serve with ham or use as a sandwich spread. Yield: 2 cups.

Remoulade Sauce

1 cup mayonnaise
⅓ cup thick, spicy steak sauce
3 tablespoons minced fresh cilantro or parsley
2 tablespoons minced fresh chives
2 tablespoons capers, drained
2 tablespoons sweet pickle relish, drained
1 tablespoon prepared mustard
¼ to ½ teaspoon hot sauce

Combine all ingredients in a medium bowl; stir well. Store in glass containers in refrigerator. Serve with seafood, roast beef, or turkey, or use as a sandwich spread. Yield: 1¾ cups.

Cranberry-Kumquat Salsa

2 cups fresh or frozen cranberries
6 kumquats or 1 small orange, peeled
2 jalapeño peppers, seeded and finely
  chopped
3 tablespoons minced crystallized ginger
¾ cup sugar
¼ cup minced fresh mint

Position slicing disc in food processor bowl; with processor running, press cranberries through food chute with food pusher, using light pressure. Transfer cranberries to a small bowl.

Coarsely chop kumquats. Position knife blade in processor bowl; add kumquats, peppers, and ginger. Pulse 3 to 5 times or until mixture is finely chopped; add to cranberries. Stir in sugar and mint. Store in glass containers in refrigerator. Serve with pork or poultry. Yield: 2 cups.

Vegetable-Olive Salsa

3 large stalks celery, cut into 3" pieces
⅔ cup pimiento-stuffed olives, rinsed and
  drained
4 banana peppers, seeded and chopped
3 green onions with tops, cut into 1" pieces
½ cup fresh cilantro or parsley
1½ cups frozen whole kernel corn, thawed
1 tablespoon olive oil
1 tablespoon lemon juice
1 teaspoon ground cumin

Position slicing disc in food processor bowl; with processor running, press celery and olives through food chute with food pusher, using light pressure. Transfer celery and olives to a medium bowl.

Position knife blade in processor bowl; add peppers, onions, and cilantro. Pulse 3 to 5 times or until vegetables are finely chopped; add to celery mixture. Stir in corn, olive oil, lemon juice, and cumin. Store in glass containers in refrigerator. Serve with tortilla chips. Yield: 3¼ cups.

Pineapple Salsa

1 (15¼-ounce) can pineapple tidbits in juice,
  drained
2 kiwifruit, peeled and chopped
1 jalapeño pepper, seeded and minced
2 tablespoons minced fresh mint
1 tablespoon minced fresh cilantro
1 teaspoon sugar
½ teaspoon ground ginger
1½ teaspoons lemon juice

Combine all ingredients in a medium bowl; stir well. Store in glass containers in refrigerator. Serve with poultry, pork, lamb, or fish. Yield: 2 cups.

Left: You can decorate the jars by wrapping kraft paper over the lids and securing it with jute. Tie on gift tags with storage and serving suggestions. For a special touch, use sealing wax and a metal stamp to make merry medallions to anchor the jute. It's easiest to make the seals on a flat surface covered with waxed paper and then hot-glue them to the jars. (For a source listing for sealing wax and stamps, see page 153.)

Darn These Napkins—And Revive a Tradition

In 18th-century Pennsylvania, every schoolgirl had to know her needlework. Once she had mastered darning socks and other articles that needed mending, she was then taught to pattern-darn to create beautiful samplers.

Today this art is being revived to make designs that look as if they have been woven into the fabric. Following a charted pattern, you create the design by working horizontal rows of straight running stitches across the fabric. Once you get the hang of this technique—and you very quickly will—you'll want to stitch a menagerie of these animal-motif napkins.

Materials for 1 napkin:
chart on page 147
purchased 12½"-square (28-count) oatmeal Heritage napkin, or (28-count) linen or evenweave napkin, hemmed to 12½" square
size 24 tapestry needle
1 (27-yard) skein each of size 5 pearl cotton: dark brown, maroon for reindeer; black, dark green for cows; rust, dark green for squirrels
thread to match fabric
liquid ravel preventer

Note: For information on ordering Heritage napkins, see source listing on page 153.

When stitching design, use 1 length of pearl cotton per design row. Determine the length of area in which design will be stitched on napkin. Referring to chart, count number of rows of each color of thread. Cut this number of lengths of thread, each 1½ times the length of design area.

Design will be worked on 2 adjacent sides of napkin. For Heritage napkin, begin stitching so that corner of design is ¼" from left and bottom edges of drawnwork. (For other 28-count napkin, begin stitching so that corner of design is 1" from left and bottom edges of napkin.)

Thread tapestry needle with 1 length of pearl cotton. Referring to chart and photograph, begin at corner of napkin and work outward. Beginning with Row 1, work horizontal straightstitches across row according to chart, with chart indicating number of vertical threads each stitch will cover. Repeat design desired number of times across napkin. At beginning and end of each row, leave a 3" tail on wrong side of napkin.

To finish off work, on wrong side of napkin, interweave thread tails where designs meet at corner.

With matching thread, machine-stitch across tails just outside completed design to secure. Trim threads just outside stitching line and apply liquid ravel preventer to raw ends of threads.

Sweet Rewards

Remember the heavenly fragrance of cinnamon and sugar wafting from the oven? A warm, fragrant kitchen is only one of the comforts of baking Christmas cookies. Other delectable dividends are sweet presents to give to friends and treats to fill your own cookie jar. Enjoy even more flavors this year by organizing a cookie exchange; to learn how, see the box on page 87.

Peanutty Chocolate-Chip Bars

1 cup all-purpose flour
⅓ cup sugar
½ cup butter or margarine, softened
½ cup sugar
¼ cup creamy peanut butter
½ cup light corn syrup
2 large eggs
1 teaspoon vanilla extract
¾ cup chopped dry-roasted peanuts
¾ cup semisweet or milk chocolate morsels

Combine first 3 ingredients in a large mixing bowl; beat at low speed of an electric mixer until mixture resembles coarse meal.

Press mixture into bottom of a lightly greased 8"-square pan. Bake at 350° for 18 to 20 minutes or until lightly browned.

Combine ½ cup sugar and next 4 ingredients; beat well at low speed of an electric mixer. Stir in peanuts and chocolate morsels.

Pour mixture over crust. Bake at 350° for 35 to 38 minutes or until filling is set and golden. If needed, cover pan with aluminum foil to prevent excessive browning. Cool completely in pan on a wire rack. Cut into bars. Yield: about 1½ dozen.

Chewy Raspberry-and-White-Chocolate Bars

2½ cups all-purpose flour
1 cup sugar
½ teaspoon ground nutmeg
1 cup chopped walnuts
⅔ cup butter or margarine, softened
2 large eggs, beaten
1 (10-ounce) jar raspberry preserves
3 ounces white chocolate, chopped

Combine first 3 ingredients in a large bowl, stirring well. Add next 3 ingredients; beat at low speed of an electric mixer until mixture resembles coarse meal.

Reserve 1½ cups crumb mixture; press remaining crumb mixture into bottom of a lightly greased 8"-square pan.

Spread raspberry preserves over crust to within ½" of edge on all sides; sprinkle white chocolate over preserves. Sprinkle reserved crumb mixture over top. Bake at 350° for 45 to 47 minutes or until lightly browned. Cool completely in pan on a wire rack. Cut into bars. Yield: 20 bars.

Left: Bounty like this makes Christmas memorable. From left to right: Granola Thumbprints, Apple-Walnut Tea Cakes, Chewy Raspberry-and-White-Chocolate Bars, Noah's Ark Cookies, Peanutty Chocolate-Chip Bars, Hazelnut-Spice Shortbread Cookies, and Triple-Chocolate Cookies.

Granola Thumbprints

1 cup butter or margarine, softened
½ cup firmly packed brown sugar
1 large egg, separated
1 teaspoon vanilla extract
½ teaspoon almond extract
1 cup all-purpose flour
2 cups regular oats, toasted
1¼ cups finely chopped pecans, almonds, or walnuts
½ cup fruit preserves or 36 milk chocolate kisses

Beat butter at medium speed of an electric mixer until creamy; gradually add sugar, beating well. Add egg yolk and vanilla and almond extracts; mix well. Add flour and oats; mix well. Refrigerate dough 30 minutes.

Shape dough into 1" balls. Beat egg white and 2 teaspoons water; dip balls in egg-white mixture and roll in pecans. Place about 2" apart on greased cookie sheets. Press thumb in each cookie to make an indentation. Bake at 300° for 15 minutes. Spoon about ½ teaspoon preserves into each indentation or fill each indentation with 1 milk chocolate kiss. Bake an additional 15 minutes. Transfer to wire racks and cool completely. Yield: about 3 dozen.

Hazelnut-Spice Shortbread Cookies

1 cup hazelnuts
1¾ cups butter, softened
1¼ cups firmly packed brown sugar
2½ cups all-purpose flour
½ cup regular oats, uncooked
1 teaspoon ground cardamom
¾ teaspoon salt

Place hazelnuts in a single layer on a baking sheet; bake at 350° for 10 to 15 minutes. Rub hazelnuts briskly with a towel to remove skins; discard skins. Coarsely chop hazelnuts and set aside.

Beat butter at medium speed of an electric mixer until creamy; gradually add sugar, beating until creamy. Combine flour and next 3 ingredients; add to creamed mixture, mixing well. Stir in chopped hazelnuts. (Dough will be stiff.)

Using about ¼ cup dough for each, form into balls. Place balls 3" to 4" apart on ungreased cookie sheets. Flatten each ball into a ¾"-thick round. Bake at 325° for 20 to 25 minutes or until lightly browned. Transfer to wire racks and cool completely. Yield: 20 cookies.

Above: Tiny aspic cutters give precise detail to these elegant Snowflake Cookies; for a source listing, see page 153.

Apple-Walnut Tea Cakes

½ cup butter or margarine, softened
1¼ cups firmly packed brown sugar
1 large egg
2 cups all-purpose flour
½ teaspoon baking soda
½ teaspoon salt
½ teaspoon ground allspice
½ cup unsweetened apple juice, divided
1 cup peeled, chopped Granny Smith apple
1 cup chopped walnuts
1 cup raisins or chopped dates
1½ cups sifted powdered sugar

Beat butter at medium speed of an electric mixer until creamy; gradually add brown sugar, beating well. Add egg; beat well. Combine flour and next 3 ingredients. To creamed mixture, alternately add flour mixture and ¼ cup apple juice, beginning and ending with flour mixture and beating well after each addition. Stir in apple, walnuts, and raisins. Drop dough by heaping tablespoonfuls onto lightly greased cookie sheets. Bake at 350° for 15 minutes or until golden. Transfer to wire racks. Combine powdered sugar and remaining ¼ cup apple juice and drizzle over warm cookies. Cool. Yield: about 3½ dozen.

Triple-Chocolate Cookies

1 (12-ounce) package semisweet chocolate
    morsels, divided
¼ cup plus 2 tablespoons butter-flavored
    shortening
½ cup sugar
2 large eggs
¼ cup all-purpose flour
¼ cup unsweetened cocoa
¼ teaspoon baking powder
¼ teaspoon salt
1 teaspoon ground cinnamon
1 cup milk chocolate morsels
1 cup chopped pecans
Pecan halves

Place 1⅓ cups semisweet chocolate morsels in top of a double boiler; bring water to a boil. Reduce heat to low; cook until chocolate melts, stirring occasionally. Cool.

Beat shortening at medium speed of an electric mixer until creamy; gradually add sugar, beating well. Add eggs and melted chocolate; beat well. Combine flour and next 4 ingredients; add flour mixture to creamed mixture, mixing well. Stir in remaining semisweet morsels, milk chocolate morsels, and chopped pecans.

Drop dough by tablespoonfuls onto greased cookie sheets; press a pecan half into each cookie. Bake at 350° for 10 minutes or until cookies look dry and cracked but feel soft when pressed gently. Cool slightly on cookie sheets; transfer to wire racks and cool completely. Yield: 40 cookies.

Noah's Ark Cookies

¼ cup plus 3 tablespoons butter or
    margarine, softened
1 (3-ounce) package cream cheese, softened
¾ cup sugar
2 tablespoons lemon juice
2¼ cups all-purpose flour
Sugar
Semisweet chocolate minimorsels

Beat butter and cream cheese at medium speed of an electric mixer until creamy; gradually add ¾ cup sugar and lemon juice, beating until creamy. Add flour to creamed mixture and beat until blended. Divide dough into thirds. Shape each portion of dough into a circle. Wrap each portion in plastic wrap and chill at least 2 hours.

Work with 1 portion of dough at a time, leaving remainder in refrigerator until ready to use. Roll dough to ¼" thickness on a lightly floured surface. Cut dough with 2½" to 3" animal-shaped cookie cutters and place shapes 2" apart on lightly greased cookie sheets. Using scraps of dough, form tails for animals by rolling small pieces of dough into thin ropes and gently pressing onto cookie shapes. Form manes by pressing pieces of dough through a clean garlic press and gently pressing strands of dough onto cookie shapes. Sprinkle cookies with sugar and press a minimorsel into each cookie to form an eye. Repeat procedure with remaining dough.

Bake at 350° for 8 to 10 minutes or until edges are lightly browned. Transfer to wire racks and cool completely. Yield: about 2 dozen.

Snowflake Cookies

Tracing paper
pattern on page 146
1 cup sugar
¾ cup butter or margarine, softened
2 large egg yolks
3 tablespoons milk
1 teaspoon vanilla extract
1 teaspoon almond extract
½ teaspoon salt
2 cups all-purpose flour
1½ cups cornstarch
Powdered sugar
Edible glitter (optional; see source listing on
**   page 153)**

Using tracing paper, trace pattern and cut out. Set aside.

Combine sugar and next 6 ingredients in a large bowl; beat at medium speed of an electric mixer until blended. Combine flour and cornstarch; add to creamed mixture, beating well. (Dough will be stiff.)

Divide dough into fourths. Working with 1 portion of dough at a time, place dough on a waxed-paper-lined, greased cookie sheet. Roll dough to ⅛" thickness. For each cookie, place pattern on dough and, using a fluted pastry wheel or sharp knife, cut out around edge of pattern. Referring to pattern and to photograph at left, use a drinking straw and a knife or tiny aspic cutters to cut decorative pattern in snowflake. Refrigerate dough 20 minutes. Lift waxed paper off cookie sheet and place on a flat work surface. Remove excess dough from between

cookie shapes. Carefully lift cookie shapes from waxed paper and place on greased cookie sheet.

Bake at 400° for 5 minutes. Cool slightly on cookie sheet. Transfer to wire racks and generously cover with sifted powdered sugar and, if desired, edible glitter. Cool completely. Repeat with remaining dough. Yield: about 2 dozen.

The Cookie Swap

You want to make *all* these delicious cookie recipes, but time is so precious during the holidays. The perfect solution? Gather your friends and have a cookie swap. Each person doubles or triples a recipe, brings the cookies to the party, and then shares them with each of the other participants. That way everyone enjoys a maximum variety of treats with minimum effort. Here's how:

•Set a date for your party about two weeks before Christmas. Or hold your party well before the busy Christmas season and freeze the cookies.

•Ask participants to make one dozen cookies per person attending. For large parties, a half dozen cookies per person should be enough. Don't forget to make extras to eat at the party.

•Making the dough or baking the cookies ahead of time is a great time-saver. Many types of cookie dough can be stored in airtight containers in the refrigerator for up to one week or frozen for up to six months. Baked cookies will keep up to eight months in the freezer. To thaw, set them out at room temperature for 10 to 15 minutes.

•Provide each guest with a large container for collecting the goodies. Decorate boxes, gift bags, or tins with stickers, ribbons or rubber-stamped designs. Line them with greaseproof paper, such as cellophane, waxed paper, or foil.

•Serve beverages and perhaps some additional snacks—but no one touches the cookies until all the containers are filled!

'Tis the Seasoning

Surprise everyone this holiday season with the novelty of a savory cheesecake, served as either an appetizer or an entrée. Similar in appearance to traditional dessert cheesecakes but not at all sweet, each of these rich and delectable cakes will draw raves.

Pesto Cheesecake

1 cup crushed wheat crackers
1 cup finely chopped walnuts, divided
¼ cup butter or margarine, melted
2 (8-ounce) packages cream cheese, softened
11 ounces crumbled feta cheese
3 large eggs
½ cup commercial pesto
2 tablespoons plus 1 teaspoon all-purpose
    flour, divided
1 (8-ounce) carton sour cream
Garnish: fresh basil sprigs, walnut halves
    (optional)
Tomato-Pepper Puree (recipe follows)

Combine crushed crackers, ½ cup walnuts, and butter; stir well. Firmly press mixture in bottom of a 9" springform pan. Set aside.

Beat cream cheese at high speed of an electric mixer until creamy. Add feta cheese and beat at medium speed until smooth. Add eggs, 1 at a time, beating well after each addition. Add pesto and 2 tablespoons flour; mix well. Stir in remaining ½ cup walnuts. Pour batter into prepared pan. Bake at 325° for 50 minutes. Combine sour cream and 1 remaining teaspoon flour; stir well. Spread sour-cream mixture on top of cheesecake; bake an additional 10 minutes. Cool to room temperature in pan on a wire rack. Serve at room temperature or cover and chill at least 8 hours.

Left: Just as fruit toppings accent traditional dessert cheesecakes, chopped vegetables and salsa complement savory Chicken-Nacho Cheesecake (top). Festive Crab-and-Muenster Cheesecake (bottom) is filled with colorful bits of chives and pimiento.

To serve, carefully remove sides of springform pan. If desired, garnish with fresh basil sprigs and walnut halves. Serve with Tomato-Pepper Puree. Yield: 1 (9") cheesecake.

Tomato-Pepper Puree

2 tablespoons olive oil
3 large sweet red peppers, coarsely chopped
1 cup seeded and chopped fresh plum tomato
2 cloves garlic, minced
1 tablespoon balsamic vinegar
½ teaspoon fresh ground pepper

Heat oil in a large skillet over medium-low heat; add red peppers, tomato, and garlic. Sauté 15 minutes or until peppers are tender. Cool.

Combine vegetables, vinegar, and pepper in container of an electric blender; cover and process until smooth. Press pepper mixture through a sieve; discard pulp. Serve at room temperature with warm cheesecake or chill and serve with chilled cheesecake. Yield: about 1 cup.

Chicken-Nacho Cheesecake

1⅔ cups finely crushed tortilla chips
¼ cup butter or margarine, melted
3 (8-ounce) packages cream cheese, softened
4 large eggs
½ cup mayonnaise
1 (1.25-ounce) package taco seasoning mix
2 tablespoons all-purpose flour
1½ cups drained and finely chopped canned
    premium chunk white chicken
1½ cups (6 ounces) shredded Colby-Jack
    cheese
1 (8-ounce) carton sour cream
Toppings: sliced ripe olives, cooked whole
    kernel corn, chopped green onions,
    chopped fresh tomato
Picante sauce or salsa

Combine tortilla chips and butter; stir well. Firmly press mixture in bottom of a 10" springform pan; set aside.

Beat cream cheese at high speed of an electric mixer until creamy. Add eggs, 1 at a time, beating well after each addition. Add mayonnaise, taco seasoning mix, and flour; beat at low speed until smooth. Stir in chicken and cheese. Pour batter into prepared pan. Bake at 325° for 55 minutes. Spread sour cream on top of cheesecake; bake an additional 10 minutes. Cool to room temperature in pan on a wire rack; cover and chill at least 8 hours.

To serve, carefully remove sides of springform pan. Arrange toppings attractively on top of cheesecake. Serve with picante sauce or salsa. Yield: 1 (10") cheesecake.

Crab-and-Muenster Cheesecake

1¼ cups fine, dry breadcrumbs
3 tablespoons butter or margarine, melted
2 (8-ounce) packages cream cheese, softened
3 large eggs
⅔ cup mayonnaise
2 tablespoons all-purpose flour
12 ounces fresh crabmeat, drained and flaked
1¼ cups (5 ounces) shredded Muenster
    cheese
¼ cup minced fresh chives
1 (2-ounce) jar diced pimiento, drained
Garnish: fresh chives (optional)

Combine breadcrumbs and butter; stir well. Firmly press crumb mixture in bottom of a 9" springform pan; set aside.

Beat cream cheese at high speed of an electric mixer until creamy. Add eggs, 1 at a time, beating well after each addition. Add mayonnaise and flour; mix until blended. Stir in crabmeat and next 3 ingredients. Pour batter into prepared pan. Bake at 325° for 1 hour or until center is completely set. Cool to room temperature in pan on a wire rack; cover and chill at least 8 hours.

To serve, carefully remove sides of springform pan. Garnish, if desired. Yield: 1 (9") cheesecake.

Note: Because this cheesecake may be frozen for

up to 2 weeks, it makes a great gift for a busy hostess. To freeze the cheesecake, cool it completely on a wire rack; carefully remove the sides of the springform pan, cover the cheesecake tightly, and freeze. Note on a gift tag accompanying the frozen cheesecake that it should be thawed in the refrigerator.

Turkey-Swiss Cheesecake

1¼ cups buttery cracker crumbs
2¼ cups (9 ounces) shredded Swiss cheese,
    divided
¼ cup butter or margarine, melted
2 (8-ounce) packages cream cheese, softened
4 large eggs
¼ cup all-purpose flour
1 (8-ounce) carton sour cream
½ teaspoon ground sage
¼ teaspoon ground white pepper
3 cups finely diced cooked turkey tenderloin
    or leftover roast turkey
Cranberry Sauce (recipe follows)

Combine cracker crumbs, ¼ cup Swiss cheese, and butter; stir well. Firmly press mixture in bottom of a 9" springform pan. Set aside.

Beat cream cheese at high speed of an electric mixer until creamy. Add eggs, 1 at a time, beating well after each addition. Add flour and next 3 ingredients; beat at low speed until smooth. Stir in remaining 2 cups Swiss cheese and turkey. Pour batter into prepared pan. Bake at 350° for 50 to 60 minutes or until center is completely set. Cool 30 minutes in pan on a wire rack.

To serve, carefully remove sides of springform pan. Serve cheesecake warm with Cranberry Sauce. Yield: 1 (9") cheesecake.

Cranberry Sauce

1 (16-ounce) can whole-berry cranberry sauce
½ cup chopped walnuts
⅓ cup finely chopped celery

Combine all ingredients in a small saucepan; cook over medium heat until thoroughly heated.

Left: Bring an Italian flair to your table with Pesto Cheesecake. Serve over a spoonful of Tomato-Pepper Puree for a tangy and eye-catching entrée.

Cranberries and Chocolate: An Inspired Duo

Traditional Christmas cranberries are luscious with rich chocolate; together, they make for divinely delicious desserts. Serve dainty Cranberry Truffles with liqueurs and coffee, or tempt the palate with Brownie-and-Cranberry Tortes (a single serving of which is shown above). Each of these spectacular desserts calls for one or more of the basic cranberry recipes on page 92.

Cranberry-Chocolate Yule Log

6 large eggs, separated
¾ cup sugar, divided
⅓ cup unsweetened cocoa
¼ teaspoon salt
½ cup whipping cream
2 tablespoons powdered sugar
½ cup Candied Cranberries (page 92)
Fudge Buttercream (recipe follows)
Garnish: Candied Cranberries

Grease a 15" x 10" x 1" jellyroll pan and line pan with waxed paper. Grease and flour waxed paper; set aside. Beat egg yolks in a large mixing bowl at high speed of an electric mixer until foamy. Gradually add ¼ cup plus 2 tablespoons sugar, beating until mixture is thick and pale. Add cocoa and beat well.

Beat egg whites and salt in a large bowl at high speed of an electric mixer until foamy. Gradually add remaining ¼ cup plus 2 tablespoons sugar, 2 tablespoons at a time, beating until stiff peaks form. Gradually fold egg-white mixture into chocolate mixture.

Spread batter evenly into prepared pan. Bake at 375° for 20 minutes or until top springs back when touched. When cake is done, immediately loosen from sides of pan; turn out onto a large cloth towel. Peel off waxed paper. Starting at 1 narrow end, roll up cake and towel together. Cool on a wire rack, seam side down.

Beat whipping cream until foamy; gradually add powdered sugar, beating until soft peaks form.

Gently fold in ½ cup Candied Cranberries.

Unroll cake; remove towel. Spread cake with whipped-cream mixture; gently reroll. Cover and chill. Spread Fudge Buttercream over cake. To represent tree bark, score frosting with the tines of a fork or a cake comb. Garnish, if desired. Yield: 10 to 12 servings.

Fudge Buttercream

⅔ cup butter, softened
2 cups sifted powdered sugar
2 ounces unsweetened chocolate, melted and cooled
1 tablespoon Grand Marnier or other orange-flavored liqueur

Beat butter at medium speed of an electric mixer until creamy; gradually add sugar, beating well. Add chocolate and Grand Marnier, beating until spreading consistency. Yield: about 1½ cups.

Cranberry Collection

Prepare scrumptious Candied Cranberries, Cranberry Coulis, and Cranberry-Chocolate Sauce to use in the recipes featured on pages 91-93.

Candied Cranberries

1 cup sugar
1 cup water
1½ cups fresh or frozen cranberries

Combine sugar and water in a saucepan. Cook over medium heat, stirring constantly, until sugar dissolves. Bring mixture to a boil and cook, without stirring, to soft ball stage (235°). Stir in cranberries and cook 4 minutes or until cranberries are coated with syrup. Drain cranberries well. Discard syrup. Arrange cranberries in a single layer on a wire rack. Cool completely. Yield: 1⅓ cups.

Cranberry Coulis

4 cups fresh or frozen cranberries
1½ cups apricot nectar
¾ cup sugar
2 tablespoons apricot brandy or crème de cassis

Combine first 3 ingredients in a large saucepan. Bring to a boil, stirring constantly, until sugar dissolves. Cover; reduce heat and simmer, stirring occasionally, 12 to 15 minutes or until cranberry mixture thickens slightly. Transfer mixture to container of an electric blender or food processor; cover and process until smooth. Stir in brandy. Cover and chill. Yield: 3⅓ cups.

Cranberry-Chocolate Sauce

¾ cup plus 2 tablespoons whipping cream
¼ cup sugar
1 cup fresh or frozen cranberries
⅓ cup crème de cassis
6 ounces bittersweet chocolate, chopped

Combine first 4 ingredients in a small saucepan. Bring to a boil, stirring constantly, until sugar dissolves. Reduce heat and simmer, uncovered, 10 to 12 minutes or until cranberries pop. Remove from heat; add chocolate and stir until smooth. Press mixture through a sieve; discard cranberry skins. Serve warm or at room temperature. Store, covered, in the refrigerator for 4 to 6 weeks. Yield: about 2 cups.

Brownie-and-Cranberry Tortes

4 ounces unsweetened chocolate, coarsely
   chopped
½ cup butter or margarine
1⅓ cups sugar
3 large eggs
¾ cup all-purpose flour
3 tablespoons unsweetened cocoa
⅔ cup Candied Cranberries (page 92)
½ teaspoon vanilla extract
Cranberry-Chocolate Sauce (page 92)
Cranberry Coulis (page 92)
Vanilla ice cream

Combine chocolate and butter in top of a double
boiler; bring water to a boil. Reduce heat to low;
cook until chocolate and butter melt, stirring occasionally. Remove from heat; transfer to a medium-
size bowl. Cool 5 minutes.

Add sugar to chocolate mixture; beat well at low
speed of an electric mixer. Add eggs, 1 at a time,
beating well after each addition. Add flour and cocoa; beat just until blended. Stir in Candied Cranberries and vanilla.

Spread batter into a greased and floured 8"-square
pan. Bake at 325° for 35 minutes or until a wooden
pick inserted in center comes out slightly creamy.
(Brownie will be lower in center than the edges.)
Cool completely in pan on a wire rack. Cover and
chill at least 8 hours.

To serve, cut brownie into 9 squares. For each
serving, spoon Cranberry-Chocolate Sauce onto a
dessert plate. Center a brownie square on sauce.
Spoon Cranberry Coulis over Chocolate Sauce in
small circles around brownie; swirl 1 edge of each
circle with the tip of a sharp knife. Top brownie
with a scoop of vanilla ice cream; drizzle additional
Cranberry-Chocolate Sauce and Cranberry Coulis
over ice cream. Serve immediately. Yield: 9 servings.

Chocolate-Cranberry Ice Cream Dessert

1 (14-ounce) can sweetened condensed milk
⅔ cup chocolate-flavored syrup
3 tablespoons unsweetened cocoa
2 cups whipping cream, whipped
¾ cup Candied Cranberries (page 92)
½ cup chopped almonds, toasted
Cranberry Coulis (page 92)
Garnish: toasted slivered almonds, Candied
   Cranberries

Combine first 3 ingredients in a large mixing
bowl; beat at low speed of an electric mixer until
smooth. Fold in whipped cream.

Pour into an 11" x 7" x 2" baking dish or other 2-
quart container; cover and freeze until partially
frozen. Stir well; fold in ¾ cup Candied Cranberries
and chopped almonds. Freeze until firm.

To serve, arrange small scoops of ice cream on individual dessert plates. Spoon Cranberry Coulis
around ice cream. Garnish, if desired. Yield: 8 to 10
servings.

Cranberry Truffles

¼ cup whipping cream
2 tablespoons powdered sugar
8 ounces bittersweet chocolate, chopped
¼ cup plus 2 tablespoons unsalted butter, cut
   into small pieces
2 tablespoons crème de cassis or Cointreau
30 Candied Cranberries (page 92)
Unsweetened cocoa *or* 10 ounces bittersweet
   chocolate plus ground toasted nuts, bits of
   Candied Cranberries, silver sprinkles
   (optional)
Paper candy cups

Combine whipping cream and sugar in a medium saucepan; bring to a boil, stirring constantly.
Add 8 ounces bittersweet chocolate and butter;
remove from heat and stir until chocolate and butter
melt. Stir in liqueur. Cover and chill 2 hours or
until firm.

Wrap mixture around each Candied Cranberry,
forming 1" balls. Roll truffles in cocoa. Place each
truffle in a paper candy cup. Store in an airtight container in refrigerator or freeze up to 3 months. Yield:
30 truffles.

Variation: To coat truffles in chocolate, prepare
truffles as directed above, except do not roll truffles
in cocoa. Place truffles on a baking sheet lined with
waxed paper; freeze until very firm.

Place 10 ounces bittersweet chocolate in top of a
double boiler; bring water to a boil. Reduce heat to
low; cook until chocolate melts, stirring frequently.
Remove from heat and stir until smooth.

Working quickly, dip each truffle into melted
chocolate. If desired, roll in ground toasted nuts, bits
of Candied Cranberries, or silver sprinkles. Place
each truffle in a paper candy cup. Store in an airtight container in refrigerator or freeze up to 3
months.

A Stenciled Cloth Sets the Table

Stencil and stitch this stunning table quilt to dress up a dining room table or drape on a sideboard. The tablecloth's reds and greens make it perfect for Christmas, while its classic quilt design allows it to be displayed in other seasons.

Materials:
stencil patterns on pages 148–49
4 (8½" x 11") sheets of frosted template plastic
craft knife
18" x 46" piece of white cardboard or heavy paper
T square and ruler
black fine-tipped permanent marker
masking tape
4 yards (45"-wide) cream-on-cream print muslin
1½ yards (54"-wide) cotton flannel or thin batting
acrylic fabric paints: red, green, yellow
3 stencil brushes
cream sewing thread
cream quilting thread

Note: Finished size of tablecloth is 50" square. Wash and press all fabrics before using. Seam allowances are ¼".

To make stencils, work on a hard surface. Trace stencil pattern onto frosted side of plastic, making a separate stencil for each paint color. Using craft knife, cut stencils on shiny side of plastic.

Use clear tape to correct cutting errors or to block out portions of design. If desired, practice stenciling on muslin scraps before beginning project. Start with largest color area and work with 1 color at a time. Allow each color to dry before stenciling next color. Periodically wash and thoroughly dry all stencils to prevent smudges. To heat-set design, press fabric on wrong side, using a press cloth and a hot, dry iron.

To make cardboard stencil guide, referring to Diagram and using T square and ruler, draw stencil guide on white piece of cardboard in dimensions indicated. Mark sashing, sashing centers, and block centers on guide. Trace over lines with black marker so that lines will show through muslin.

From muslin, cut 2 (42") squares for top and backing, 2 (9" x 42") strips for side borders, and 2 (9" x 50½") strips for top and bottom borders. From flannel, cut 1 (50") square for batting.

To mark center of fabric, fold top in half horizontally and then vertically; finger-press. Do not use pencil to mark fabric; mark with straight pin.

Using masking tape, tape stencil guide to a smooth work surface. Place tablecloth top right side up over guide, aligning center of top with center of guide. Tape top to work surface to secure.

To stencil top, begin by stenciling middle 3-block section. Referring to Diagram and using cardboard stencil guide showing through fabric for placement, align center of sashing stencil with center of horizontal sashing A. Working from center outward, begin stenciling sashing A, stenciling green half-diamonds first. Where horizontal sashing abuts vertical sashing E and F, use tape to block out portion of stencil so diamond motif abuts vertical sashing. Repeat to stencil red inner diamonds of sashing, using tape to block out last diamond on each end as needed. Repeat for horizontal sashing B.

Stencil vertical sashing C and D as above, using tape to block out design as needed so that diamond motif abuts horizontal sashing A and B. Stencil vertical sashing E and F, beginning with center of stencil aligned with top of sashing A and working downward. Do not block out end of design at bottom of block, as design will be continued later.

Referring to Diagram and using cardboard stencil guide for placement, center and stencil oak leaf and rose in middle 3 blocks.

Untape top from work surface and move it down over stencil guide, aligning center and guidelines for upper 3 blocks. Tape top to work surface.

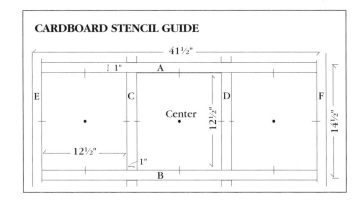

CARDBOARD STENCIL GUIDE

Stencil upper sashing and vertical sashing as above, continuing vertical sashing E and F from center. Use tape to block out top of vertical sashing E and F to square corner of sashing (see photograph). Stencil blocks as above.

Untape top from work surface and move it up over guide, aligning center and guidelines for lower 3 blocks. Stencil sashing and blocks as above. Let dry; then heat-set.

For side borders, fold 1 (9" x 42") strip in half lengthwise and press. Unfold; mark widthwise center of border strip. Tape border strip to work surface. Measure and mark 1" from each end of strip. Aligning border stencil with fold line as indicated on pattern, stencil border, working from center outward. Do not stencil beyond marked line, so that border motif ends ¾" outside of seam allowance. Repeat for other side border.

For top and bottom borders, mark center of 1 (9" x 50½") strip as above. Tape border to work surface. Measure and mark 4½" from each end to allow for

corner border motif. Stencil border as above, not stenciling beyond marked area. For corner motif, referring to photograph, center rose-and-diamond pattern from block design within marked areas and stencil. Repeat for remaining border. Let borders dry; then heat-set.

To attach borders, with right sides facing and raw edges aligned, stitch side borders to each side of top; then attach top and bottom borders in same manner. Press seams toward sashing.

Center and stack backing (right side down), batting, and top (right side up). Working from center outward, baste through all layers to secure.

Turn long raw edge of side border strip under ¼" and press. Fold strip in half to backing and slipstitch pressed edge of border to backing. Repeat for opposite side. Fold and press top and bottom borders in same manner, tucking excess inside ends of border to square corners. Slipstitch folded edges closed.

Using quilting thread, outline-quilt along all sashing lines and ⅛" from outside edge of borders.

95

An After-the-Show Buffet

Whether it's your annual foray to The Nutcracker *ballet or your child's dramatic debut in the school play, this star-quality dinner is a grand finale. The dishes can be made ahead and then quickly assembled for a show-stopping presentation.*

Menu

Blue Cheese Dip with Red and Green Dippers

Herbed Mushroom Pastries

◆

Spiked Honey-Orange Ham

Acorn Squash with Dates and Walnuts

Fresh Spinach Salad with Dijon Vinaigrette

Commercial Crusty Hard Rolls

Sparkling Mineral Water

◆

Suggested Wines:
Merlot or Beaujolais-Villages

◆

Homemade Lemon Ice Cream

Commercial Sugar Cookies

Coffee

Serves 10

Blue Cheese Dip with Red and Green Dippers

1 (8-ounce) carton sour cream
1 cup mayonnaise
4 ounces blue cheese, crumbled
1 teaspoon dried basil
¼ teaspoon garlic salt
½ cup sliced almonds, toasted and chopped
Small cherry tomatoes
Broccoli flowerets
Sliced cucumber
Julienned sweet red pepper

Combine first 3 ingredients in a medium bowl; stir well. Stir in basil and garlic salt; cover and chill thoroughly.

Just before serving, stir in toasted almonds, reserving 2 tablespoons to sprinkle on top. Serve with cherry tomatoes, broccoli, cucumber, and red pepper. Yield: 2½ cups.

Herbed Mushroom Pastries

3 slices bacon
1 cup finely chopped onion
2 cloves garlic, minced
1 pound fresh mushrooms, sliced
2 tablespoons Worcestershire sauce
1 teaspoon lemon juice
½ teaspoon dried rosemary, crushed
¼ teaspoon dried basil
¼ teaspoon salt
⅛ teaspoon pepper
2 tablespoons chopped fresh parsley
¼ cup plus 1 tablespoon Italian-seasoned breadcrumbs
18 sheets frozen phyllo pastry, thawed
1¼ cups butter or margarine, melted or butter-flavored vegetable cooking spray

Cook bacon in a large skillet until crisp; remove bacon, reserving 1 tablespoon drippings in skillet.

Crumble bacon and set aside. Sauté onion and garlic in drippings, stirring constantly, until tender. Add mushrooms and next 6 ingredients; sauté 10 to 12 minutes or until all liquid has evaporated and mushrooms are tender. Stir in parsley, breadcrumbs, and reserved bacon.

Cut each sheet of phyllo lengthwise into 6 strips. Working with 1 strip at a time, brush each strip lightly with melted butter or spray lightly with cooking spray. Stack 2 strips together. Keep remaining phyllo covered with a slightly damp towel. Place about 1 teaspoon mushroom mixture at base of phyllo strip; fold the right bottom corner over to form a triangle. Continue folding back and forth into

97

a triangle to end of strip. Repeat procedure with remaining phyllo strips, melted butter, and mushroom mixture.

Place triangles, seam side down, on lightly greased baking sheets. Bake at 375° for 20 minutes or until golden. Serve warm. Yield: 4½ dozen.

Note: Herbed Mushroom Pastries may be frozen up to 4 weeks before baking. To bake, follow instructions above.

Spiked Honey-Orange Ham

1 (9- to 10-pound) smoked, fully cooked
    ham half
Whole cloves
¼ cup Cointreau or other orange-flavored
    liqueur
1 cup honey
2 tablespoons frozen orange juice
    concentrate, thawed
¼ teaspoon ground cinnamon
¼ teaspoon ground cloves
Garnish: fresh crab apples, kale leaves

Slice away skin from ham. Score fat on ham in a diamond design and stud with cloves. Fill the injector needle of a bulb baster with Cointreau and inject into ham in several places. Place ham, fat side up, on a rack in a shallow roasting pan. Insert meat thermometer into thickest part of ham, making sure it does not touch fat or bone.

Cover and bake at 325° for 1½ hours. Combine honey and next 3 ingredients in a small bowl; stir well. Uncover ham and brush exposed portion of ham with honey mixture. Bake, uncovered, an additional hour or until thermometer registers 140°, basting frequently with honey mixture. Transfer ham to a serving platter. Garnish, if desired. Let stand at least 25 minutes before slicing. Yield: 10 servings.

Note: Bulb basters with injector needle attachments can be found at most kitchen supply stores. Ham can be baked a day in advance and refrigerated. Let come to room temperature before serving.

Acorn Squash with Dates and Walnuts

5 small acorn squash
1 (8-ounce) package chopped dates
½ cup chopped walnuts
1 teaspoon grated orange rind
½ cup orange juice
⅓ cup red currant jelly
3 tablespoons butter or margarine
Garnish: lemon rind curls

Cut squash in half crosswise; remove and discard seeds. Place squash halves, cut side up, in a 15" x 10" x 1" jelly-roll pan. Combine dates and walnuts; spoon into squash cavities.

Combine orange rind and next 3 ingredients in a small saucepan. Cook over medium heat until jelly and butter melt; spoon into squash cavities. Bake, covered, at 350° for 1 hour or until squash is tender. Garnish, if desired. Yield: 10 servings.

Note: To make ahead, squash may be baked for 30 minutes and refrigerated up to 24 hours. Bake an additional 30 minutes before serving.

Fresh Spinach Salad with Dijon Vinaigrette

½ cup olive oil
¼ cup red wine vinegar
¼ cup minced fresh parsley
3 tablespoons Dijon mustard
¼ teaspoon salt
¼ teaspoon pepper
1 pound fresh spinach
1 purple onion, thinly sliced
4 hard-cooked egg yolks, finely chopped

Combine first 6 ingredients in a jar; cover tightly and shake vigorously. Chill at least 3 hours.

Remove stems from spinach; wash leaves thoroughly and pat dry. Tear into bite-size pieces. Combine spinach and onion in a large bowl. Just before serving, pour dressing over salad and toss gently. Sprinkle with egg yolk. Yield: 10 servings.

Homemade Lemon Ice Cream

1 cup sugar
¼ cup all-purpose flour
½ teaspoon salt
4 large eggs, lightly beaten
4 cups milk
3 cups whipping cream
2 tablespoons grated lemon rind
1 cup fresh lemon juice
1 cup sifted powdered sugar
Commercial sugar cookies

Combine first 3 ingredients; stir well. Place eggs in a medium saucepan; gradually add sugar mixture and milk, stirring well with a wire whisk. Cook over medium heat, stirring frequently, 15 minutes or until mixture thickens and coats a metal spoon. Remove from heat and cool completely. Cover and chill mixture thoroughly.

Combine whipping cream, lemon rind, lemon juice, and powdered sugar; stir well. Add whipping-cream mixture to chilled custard; stir well. Pour mixture into freezer container of a 1-gallon hand-turned or electric freezer. Freeze according to manufacturer's instructions. Pack freezer with additional ice and salt, and let stand 1 to 2 hours before serving. Serve with sugar cookies. Yield: 11½ cups.

Design a Buffet That Goes with the Flow

Even for a small party such as this, the thoughtful hostess will arrange the dinnerware, beverages, and food so that her guests can negotiate the buffet table with ease.

To cut down on congestion, place the various courses in different locations. Serve the appetizers from a coffee table and end tables and the main course from a sideboard. After dinner, set up the dessert on an occasional table.

Juggling plates, cutlery, and drinks can be tricky. Stack plates at the beginning of the buffet and cutlery and napkins (preferably bundled together) at the end. Consider serving the beverages from a separate table or sideboard. That way, guests can simply set their plates down and come back to retrieve their glasses.

Ideas

Potables with a Past

*Syllabub, shrub, glogg, and wassail—
even the names of these beverages
sound quaint. Indeed, these drinks have
been part of festive occasions for
centuries. Happily, the recipes given
here are updated for modern cooks.*

Syllabub

1 quart whipping cream
1½ cups milk
⅔ cup Sauternes or other sweet white wine
¾ cup sugar
1 teaspoon vanilla extract
Freshly grated nutmeg

Combine first 5 ingredients in a large bowl;
beat at medium speed of an electric mixer until
frothy. Pour into chilled cups and sprinkle with
nutmeg. Serve immediately. Yield: 8 cups.

*Above: Like many of our culinary Christmas traditions,
syllabub originated in merry old England. This thick, frothy
drink was customarily served in special syllabub cups, but
you could use demitasse cups or pots de crème.*

*Left: Wassail has long been
associated with festivity and
good wishes. The proper
container for steaming wassail
is a wassail bowl. An heirloom
punch bowl will work, but even
a humble mixing bowl looks
great when dressed up with a
grapevine wreath, sprigs of
greenery, and an apple-red
bow. As a final touch, mold a
tablespoon of butter mixture to
resemble a tiny apple and
insert a clove for a stem; place
a butter "apple" in a cup, pour
in the drink, and serve.*

Hot Buttered Wassail

2 quarts apple cider
2 cups ginger ale
2 cups unsweetened orange juice
1 (3-ounce) package orange-pineapple-
 flavored gelatin
½ cup lemon juice
1 lemon, sliced and studded with whole cloves
2 small apples, halved lengthwise
3 (3") sticks cinnamon
½ cup butter, softened
¼ cup firmly packed brown sugar
¼ cup maple syrup

Combine first 8 ingredients in a large Dutch oven; stir well. Bring mixture to a boil; reduce heat and simmer, covered, 30 minutes.

Beat butter at medium-high speed of an electric mixer until creamy; gradually add brown sugar and maple syrup, beating until creamy. Use butter mixture immediately or cover and chill. Before using, let butter return to room temperature.

To serve, place 1 heaping tablespoon butter mixture into individual mugs; fill with hot wassail and stir well. Serve immediately. Yield: 3¼ quarts.

Sparkling Cranberry Shrub

½ cup lemon juice
¼ cup honey
1 (48-ounce) jar cranberry juice cocktail,
 chilled
1 (12-ounce) can frozen orange juice
 concentrate, thawed and undiluted
1½ cups cold water
3 (12-ounce) cans lemon-lime carbonated
 beverage, chilled

Combine lemon juice and honey in a punch bowl; stir well. Stir in next 3 ingredients. Just before serving, stir in lemon-lime beverage. Serve over crushed ice. Yield: 3¾ quarts.

Right: During colonial times, shrubs were spiked with liquor; today, these chilled fruity beverages are usually nonalcoholic. To add interest to your holiday buffet, serve this refreshing cranberry-flavored shrub in a selection of complementary but mismatched stemmed glasses.

Glogg

1 (2-ounce) package slivered almonds,
 toasted
½ cup raisins
½ cup golden raisins
1¾ cups brandy, divided
1 (25.4-ounce) bottle Burgundy or other dry
 red wine
3 cups unsweetened apple juice
¾ cup firmly packed brown sugar
4 (3") sticks cinnamon
3 whole nutmegs, cracked in half
2 medium oranges, quartered and studded
 with whole cloves

Combine first 3 ingredients in a small bowl; add ¾ cup brandy. Cover and let stand overnight.

Combine Burgundy and next 5 ingredients in a large Dutch oven; stir well. Bring mixture to a boil; reduce heat and simmer, uncovered, 15 minutes. Stir in remaining 1 cup brandy and simmer 3 to 5 minutes. Remove from heat and discard oranges, cinnamon, and nutmeg.

To serve, spoon about 1 tablespoon soaked-raisin mixture into individual cups; fill with hot glogg. Serve immediately. Yield: 6 cups.

Projects using children's art are on pages 104–9.

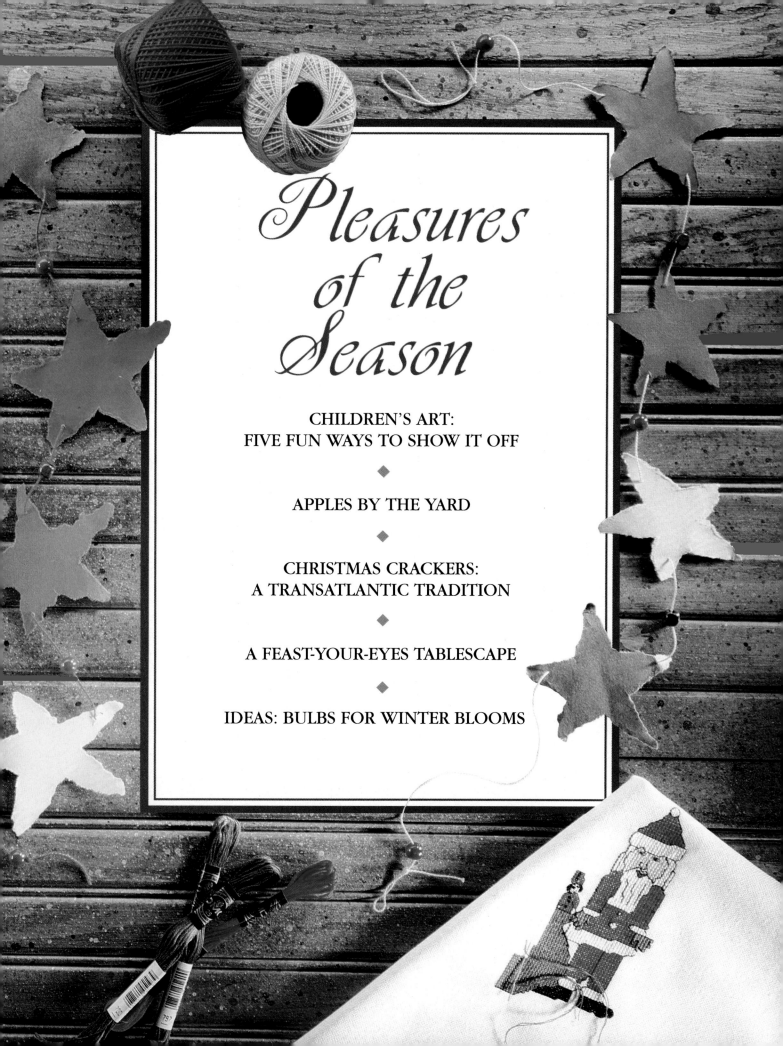

Pleasures of the Season

Children's Art:
Five Fun Ways to Show It Off

Children's artwork has long been displayed on refrigerator galleries across the country. Take your children's talents to new heights by turning their creations into wearables, gifts, plates, and decorations. Instructions for these projects begin on page 108.

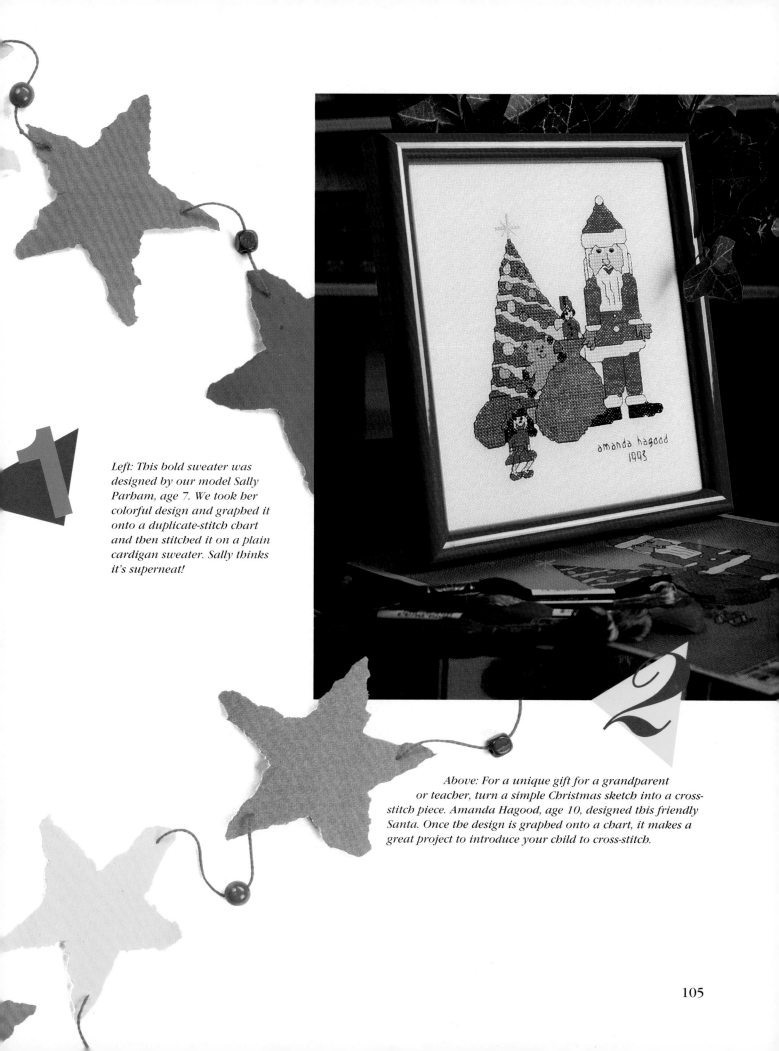

Left: This bold sweater was designed by our model Sally Parham, age 7. We took her colorful design and graphed it onto a duplicate-stitch chart and then stitched it on a plain cardigan sweater. Sally thinks it's superneat!

Above: For a unique gift for a grandparent or teacher, turn a simple Christmas sketch into a cross-stitch piece. Amanda Hagood, age 10, designed this friendly Santa. Once the design is graphed onto a chart, it makes a great project to introduce your child to cross-stitch.

3

Above: If presentation makes the package, this wrap takes the prize. Kids will have a ball coming up with interesting stamps to make their own distinctive wrapping papers.

4

106

Deck the Halls with Children's Art

Michael Sorenson, age 8, might seem young to be a regular contributor to an art gallery. But ask his mom, Kay, curator and biggest fan of Michael's artwork, and she'll tell you differently. An elementary-school art teacher for 26 years, Kay thinks that her own children's art has more prestige than any major piece of art she's ever purchased.

Kay's other two children, Michaela, 10, and Anna, 14, also contribute to Mom's "gallery"—located in the entryway, the dining room, and the formal living room of the Sorensons' Victorian home in Oak Park, Illinois. Kay rotates her children's artwork with existing pieces. "I'll take a large framed piece right off the wall and replace it with a drawing brought home from school," she says. She also has special creations that are brought out every year at Christmas as artistic remembrances from when her children were younger.

The dolls and soldiers shown draping the doorway at right were a family collaboration. But the Sorensons' is not the only home in Oak Park bedecked in the oversized decorations. Many of Kay's students live nearby, and their houses are also dressed up inside and out with giant paper nutcrackers that Kay helped them make in her class at school.

The figures are made from large sheets of construction paper. Kay provides a few patterns for the kids to trace, but basically the children come up with the designs on their own.

"Time goes by so fast when they're young, and their artwork changes dramatically. I like to have permanent reminders of the kids at every stage," says Kay.

Left: This plate was created from a picture that 5-year-old Emma O'Hagan drew for her mom and dad. The drawing was sent off to a company that turns children's artwork into dishware.

Above: Enlist neighborhood children to create multiples of stars to festoon the house with these bright garlands. The stars were drawn freehand onto construction paper and then torn out, but scissors might be easier to use.

107

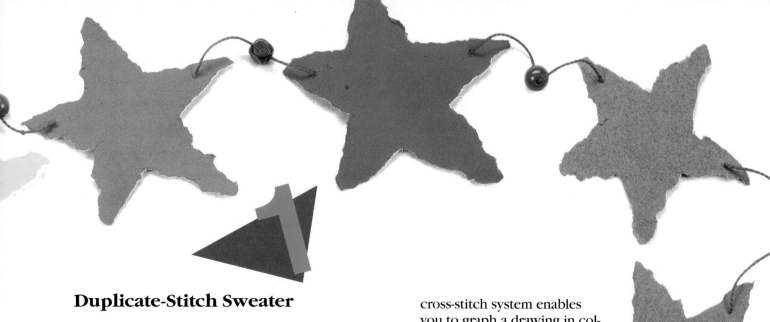

Duplicate-Stitch Sweater

To order the graphing tools needed for this project, see the source listing on page 153. The Graph-It duplicate-stitch system enables you to graph a drawing in color onto a plastic chart designed specifically for duplicate stitch. The system includes complete instructions, a graphing ruler, and graphs of various sizes, so you can accurately chart the design for sweaters of different gauges.

Follow the manufacturer's instructions to graph the drawing onto the chart. Follow the graphed chart and the Diagrams below to stitch the design onto the sweater. If desired, use colored novelty buttons to add dimension to the sweater, as we did for the snowman's nose and the star and ornaments on the tree. To personalize it even further, stitch the child's signature at the bottom of the sweater.

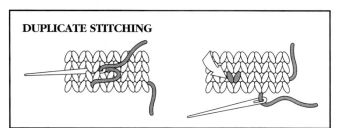

DUPLICATE STITCHING

Cross-stitch Picture

To order the graphing tools needed for this project, see the source listing on page 153. The Graph-It cross-stitch system enables you to graph a drawing in color onto a plastic chart designed just for cross-stitch. The system includes plastic graphing materials in a variety of sizes and complete instructions for charting the design.

Follow the manufacturer's instructions to graph the drawing onto the chart; then stitch it onto the desired fabric. Finish as desired. If framing, consider framing the work without glass so that the texture and quality of the stitches are not obscured.

This technique can be used to make a pillow for Dad or a framed piece to display in your office. Budding artists will get even more satisfaction out of this project if they stitch their pieces themselves.

Stamped Wrapping Paper

Make spirited wrapping paper with butcher or kraft paper, acrylic paints, and items found in your kitchen. Cookie cutters, fruits, and vegetables make festive, textural designs.

For the fruit-stamped paper shown, slice apples or oranges in half and use the cut sides for the stamps. For a roselike stamp, cut off the bottom three inches of a celery bunch; use the cut side of the bottom portion for the stamp.

Cover a flat work surface with newspaper and spread white butcher paper or brown kraft paper on top. (You and your children may want to wear smocks to protect your clothes.) Pour some acrylic paint into a paper plate and dip the stamp into the paint. Stamp the fruit or cookie cutter onto the paper in the desired pattern. Let the paint dry.

Cut out some of the designs at the end of the paper to make matching gift tags. Then wrap presents with your custom papers.

Top off the packages with bright ribbon that adds punch to the package. You can also use this same technique to perk up plain cardboard gift boxes.

Art Plate

To order the kit needed to make your art plate, see the source listing on page 153. Makit Products, Inc., will send you the complete Make-A-Plate kit.

Following the manufacturer's instructions and using watercolor markers, have your child draw a picture on the paper disc enclosed in the kit. Send the picture to Makit Products in the envelope enclosed in the kit. (The original artwork will not be returned to you.) In about six weeks, the

company will mail you a 10-inch, dishwasher-safe melamine plate.

These plates are excellent gifts for relatives or to cherish for yourself. Set out one with several cookies for Santa to enjoy on his annual visit. Make one every year for a memory gallery of your children's Christmas artwork. Hang them on a wall or use them for everyday dinnerware.

Paper Star Garland

Draw three-inch stars on sheets of colored construction paper. Either tear or cut out stars along the lines. Thread a large-eyed, blunt-tipped tapestry needle with desired length of pearl cotton. Beginning and ending with wooden beads, alternate beads and stars on the pearl cotton. Tie large knots at each end to secure.

This is a fun after-school project for kids. These cheerful stars look great anywhere a swag of color is needed—over a guest-bath mirror, across the mantel, or tied around a special present for a teacher. If desired, spray-paint a grapevine wreath white and weave the star garland among the twigs for a front-door welcome from your kids.

A Treat for the Whole Family in Old Town Spring

Hunting for gifts to tuck under the tree is a perennial part of Christmas. At Old Town Spring, Texas—one of America's many outdoor retail villages—a warm, friendly atmosphere coaxes everyone into the shopping spirit.

All year round, visitors are charmed by Old Town Spring's restored Victorian cottages and brick streets, which evoke the grace and hospitality of a bygone era.

But as Christmas approaches, Old Town Spring really comes alive. In early November an official lighting ceremony ushers in a month-long celebration called "Home for the Holidays." Throughout the season, special events, street performers and musicians, and the more than 125 wonderful shops make sure that shopping is fun for the whole family. (For other shopping villages that put on the ritz for Christmas, see the box on page 112.)

Many of the gift shops carry country crafts such as quilts, embroidered linens, colorful rag rugs, and hand-woven baskets. Children love watching candlemakers create intricate carvings from wax, while crafters amass shopping bags full of potpourri, dried flowers, lace, quilt fabrics, and cross-stitch supplies.

Other stores offer apparel in styles ranging from country and western to classic Victorian and novelty

A wealth of specialty shops provide gifts for everyone from Grandpa to the family pet.

artwear. Mothers and daughters try on matching handmade outfits to wear to holiday parties, and doting aunts select sweetly smocked dresses for their nieces. For anyone planning a Christmas wedding, there's even a bridal shop that can make a custom gown and veil.

Friends out for a day's shopping crowd the

galleries featuring American and Southwestern arts and artifacts; pottery, Indian sculptures and jewelry, and watercolors by regional artists make great gifts. Children cajole grandparents into taking a turn through toy stores overflowing with dolls, hobby horses, and kites. Specialty food shops entice gourmands who can't resist a peek at the culinary gadgets and mouthwatering array of treats to eat.

For those who find that their shopping stamina is flagging, several cafés offer reviving cups of British tea and French pastries. Mom and Dad may even enjoy a sip or two at a tasting room for Texas wines.

In the process of crossing off every item on their shopping lists, visitors can relax and enjoy a wide variety of entertainers, both amateur and professional. Cloggers dance near a 20-foot natural fir tree that is decorated for Christmas. Along the shady streets carolers stroll among handbell choirs, guitarists, and dulcimer players. And storytellers and clowns fascinate the kids while they wait to visit Santa Claus, the ultimate holiday shopper.

From Texas memorabilia to Tiffany lamps, Old Town Spring has gift ideas for collectors of all ages. Ceramic figurines for Grandmother or popular sports cards for avid athletes—these and other collectibles are found in the myriad of specialty shops that make shopping at Old Town Spring an adventure.

Local performers and appealing window displays amuse and refresh even the weariest shoppers.

When it comes to the perfect Christmas gift, some people know exactly what to bestow.

Shopping Historic U.S.A.

Many historic districts across the country offer terrific holiday shopping. For more information about villages near you, contact the following organizations:

Old Town Spring Association
123-E Midway
Spring, TX 77373
1-800-OLD TOWN (653-8696)
    or (713) 353-9310

Howard County Tourism
    Council, Inc.
P.O. Box 9
Ellicott City, MD 21041
1-800-288-TRIP (8747)

Parke County Convention
    and Visitors Bureau
P.O. Box 165
Rockville, IN 47872
(317) 569-5226

Old Washington, Inc.
Box 227
Washington, KY 41096
(606) 759-7411

Fort Bragg-Mendocino Coast
    Chamber of Commerce
P.O. Box 1141
Fort Bragg, CA 95437
(707) 961-6300

A Card Full of Wishful Whiskers

Let this winsome kitty send your best holiday wishes. Since the design is attached with pressure-sensitive glue, the recipient can gently lift it from the card and then enjoy it as a hanging ornament.

Materials:
patterns on page 150
tracing paper
1 (6" x 7") piece of white medium-weight paper
scrap of black medium-weight paper
1 (4" x 6") piece of green lightweight paper
scraps of lightweight paper: red, yellow
small sharp scissors
glue stick
5½" length of gold metallic thread
1 (7" x 10¼") piece of blue medium-weight paper
pressure-sensitive glue
1 sheet of white writing paper (optional)
5¼" x 7¼" envelope

Using tracing paper, transfer all patterns except garland to paper. Using scissors, cut out pieces and set aside.

Transfer garland pattern to tracing paper, but do not cut it out. Fold green paper in half widthwise. Lay tracing paper on green paper, aligning fold lines. Cut through all 3 layers at once. Open garland carefully and press for a few minutes under a heavy book.

Referring to photograph and pattern for placement and using glue stick, glue ledge, cat, and garland to window. Glue bows to garland.

To hang star from center pane, cut a 1½" piece from thread. Glue stars together with 1 end of thread sandwiched in between stars. Glue other end of thread to back of window at top center. Or, if desired, glue star to garland as shown.

To make hanging loop, fold remaining length of thread in half and glue ends to back of window at top center.

To make card, fold blue paper in half widthwise. Using pressure-sensitive glue, follow manufacturer's instructions to glue design to front of card. If desired, fold writing paper in half widthwise and trim to fit inside card. Glue writing paper inside card.

Apples by the Yard

These appealing apples will be the quickest and easiest ornaments you make all year. Simply twist plaid ribbon around a Styrofoam ball, add a stem, and hang your bright new apple on the tree. Select ribbons with a strong vertical stripe—it will divert attention from the widthwise stripes that won't match.

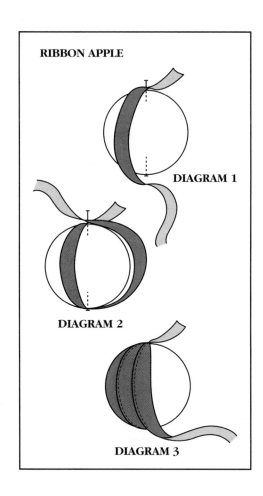

RIBBON APPLE

DIAGRAM 1

DIAGRAM 2

DIAGRAM 3

Materials for 1 apple:
1 (3"-diameter) Styrofoam ball
straight pins
3 yards (⅞"-wide) plaid ribbon (see note below)
½"-wide brown florist's tape
2 (2¼") velvet florist's leaves with wires
wire cutters

Note: Use ribbon from ½"- to 1½"-wide; yardage requirements will be greater for narrower ribbon and less for wider ribbon.

Mark top and bottom of Styrofoam ball with pins. Make a tight, 180° clockwise twist in ribbon about 1½" from 1 end; pin twist to top of ball, leaving tail of ribbon free. Referring to Diagram 1, wrap ribbon to bottom of ball and twist ribbon 180° clockwise;

pin to secure twist. Then wrap ribbon to top of ball, twist ribbon, and pin to complete first round. (See Diagram 2.)

Referring to Diagram 3, continue wrapping and twisting ribbon around ball, overlapping right edge of previous round ⅛" at equator of ball with left edge of current round. To reduce bulk at top and bottom, use pins only as needed after first round.

End last round at top of ball; twist ribbon and pin, leaving 2" tail. Trim both tails at 45° angle. To make stem, starting at top of ball and holding tails together as 1, tightly wrap florist's tape twice around tails. Referring to photograph, place leaves on top of apple, align wire with tails, and wrap tape around wire and tails to form 2" stem. Trim excess wire with wire cutters. For hanger, form a hook in end of stem.

Above: Members of one of two Birmingham chapters of the Daughters of the British Empire celebrate the success of their fund-raiser. Sheila Miller-Shugerman (far left), Jean Dunston (far right), hostess Gloria Steiner (standing), and friends demonstrate the proper way to crack a cracker.

Christmas Crackers: A Transatlantic Tradition

For the British, Christmas without crackers wouldn't seem like Christmas at all. So a group of British women now living in Birmingham, Alabama, came up with a way to have their crackers and help others, too.

Invented in the 1840s by a London confectioner, crackers are a traditional part of a British family's Christmas dinner. Before the meal, two tablemates grasp opposite ends of one cracker and pull hard. With a satisfyingly loud "crack," the crackers burst, scattering trinkets, mottoes, and brightly colored party hats.

Years ago the members of the Birmingham chapter of the Daughters of the British Empire (DBE), an association of expatriate Englishwomen, found that crackers were often difficult or even impossible to find in the United States. So in 1984, the group hit upon the clever idea of making and selling their own.

Their plan had two advantages. The profits would go to Mountbatten House, a nursing home supported by the DBE—a cause shining with the true spirit of Christmas. And, of course, the women could make a few extra crackers to set aside for their families' holiday celebrations. Christmas would seem like Christmas after all.

That first fund-raiser was so successful that the chapter has made and sold crackers every Christmas since. And as founding member Sheila Miller-Shugerman explains, the project is a year-round endeavor. Members meet monthly in each others' homes to talk, have tea, and make as many crackers as possible, since well over 3,000 of them are sold each year. "Fortunately," reports longtime member Jean Dunston, "when the conversation skips along, so do all our

fingers, and we can make a good many crackers in a single afternoon."

Gloria Steiner reveals that the secret behind the cracking sound of a cracker is a paper strip called a "snap," which the Birmingham group must import from England. Extending through the center of the cracker from end to end, the snap is actually made of two strips whose ends overlap in the center and are secured by a rough-textured substance. When the cracker is pulled apart, the friction produces a sharp cracking sound—and that's why a cracker is called a cracker.

After the crackers are sold and the holiday season winds down, the group gathers once more at a dinner party held on Twelfth Night, January 6. Here they celebrate friendship, the joy of giving, and the transatlantic transfer of traditions large and small—including, of course, the Christmas cracker, which can be found on every plate.

Crackerjack Crackers

The Christmas cracker is a British tradition that is catching on in the U.S.

Around the holidays some mail-order catalogs offer boxed sets of these gaily colored favors. Each cracker usually contains tiny trinkets or games, the obligatory crepe-paper party hat, and a slip of paper containing a pun or witty motto.

The possibilities become really interesting when you make your own crackers and personalize the contents for each guest. For the budding attorney you can include a few lawyer jokes; for the student of ballet, a silver charm in the shape of ballet slippers. Because a cracker's essential ingredient—the snap—is nearly impossible to buy in the U.S., you'll find it easier to make your crackers from a kit.

For information on both ready-made crackers and kits, see the source listings on page 153.

Garnish With Appeal

Easy and elegant, flavorful Candied Citrus Peel perks up standard fare and makes a unique gift. Shown at right, it tops off a quick dessert of purchased poundcake and chocolate sauce. From the leftover citrus you can prepare Fruit with Ginger-Rum Custard or your favorite fruit salad.

Candied Citrus Peel

2 oranges, 4 lemons, 4 limes, or
  1 large grapefruit
1 cup sugar, divided
3 tablespoons water

Working over a small bowl to catch juice, remove peel from desired fruit, using a sharp paring knife; reserve fruit and juice for another use. Cut pith away from peel. Cut peel into ⅛"-wide strips.

Combine ½ cup sugar and water in a 1-quart casserole; microwave at HIGH 1½ minutes. Stir in peel. Microwave at HIGH 6 to 8 minutes, stirring every 2 minutes, or until peel is tender.

Place remaining ½ cup sugar in a pie plate. Remove fruit peel from casserole with a slotted spoon, draining well. Add peel to pie plate in batches and toss with sugar until well coated. Place in a single layer on waxed paper; let stand at room temperature 1 hour or until dry. Store in an airtight container. Yield: 1⅓ cups.

Fruit with Ginger-Rum Custard

4 oranges or 2 large grapefruit, peeled
2 kiwifruit, peeled and sliced
1 large banana, sliced
1 cup sliced fresh strawberries
2 egg yolks
¼ cup sugar
1 tablespoon light rum
¼ teaspoon ground ginger
Garnishes: Candied Citrus Peel, toasted
  coconut

Working over a small bowl to catch juice, section oranges or grapefruit. Place sections in a large bowl; set aside. Add water to juices, if necessary, to measure ¼ cup; set aside.

Combine citrus sections, kiwifruit, banana, and strawberries; toss gently. Cover and chill.

Combine reserved juices, egg yolks, sugar, rum, and ginger in top of a double boiler. Beat at low speed of an electric mixer until well blended. Place over simmering water; continue beating at medium speed 3 to 5 minutes or until mixture has tripled in volume.

To serve, spoon fruit evenly into 4 individual stemmed dessert dishes. Spoon warm custard evenly over fruit; garnish with Candied Citrus Peel and toasted coconut. Yield: 4 servings.

Peel Possibilities

Whether you make Candied Citrus Peel for yourself or as a gift, the following are just a few of its many uses.

Gift Ideas:
  •For a zesty hostess gift, alternate layers of peel with gingersnaps in a decorative glass jar.
  •For a festive party favor at each table setting, wrap a batch of Candied Citrus Peel in bright squares of tulle and tie with silk cords, as in the photograph at right.
  •Mix ⅓ cup peach preserves with ½ cup Candied Citrus Peel and 1½ tablespoons minced crystallized ginger for a quick and delicious marmalade.

Serving Suggestions:
  •Sprinkle on ham during the last 10 minutes of baking.
  •Add to a spinach salad.
  •Garnish a sweet potato casserole or a lemon meringue or Key lime pie.
  •Place on sugar cookies before baking, or mince and stir into dough.
  •Spoon softly whipped cream around a serving of fruitcake; sprinkle on top of cream.
  •Scatter around a scoop of sorbet or sherbet and drizzle with citrus-flavored liqueur.

Above: To complete this mouth-watering arrangement, add cut vegetable dippers, assorted cheeses and crackers, and other finger foods to the vegetable foundation. For information on Kathy G's catering services, see the source listing on page 153.

A Feast-Your-Eyes Tablescape

This tablescape functions as both a lush centerpiece and a bountiful spread. Birmingham caterer Kathy G. Mezrano created it for a party of 12. For her guide to purchasing the vegetables, see the list on page 151.

Building the Base

A coffee table provides a convenient location for the appetizer buffet. To build the foundation for the vegetables, begin by positioning large serving pieces. To protect the table surface, select a piece for the front that will cover a large area. Or, if desired, cover the table with plastic wrap. Later you can tuck the excess edges of the wrap underneath the vegetables.

A simple holiday decoration adds a personal touch to the arrangement.

Choose a variety of bowls, baskets, and platters to lend textural interest.

Use a large breadboard or cutting board in the front to hold the cheeses, spreads, and crackers.

Stack serving pieces at the back of the table to add height to the arrangement for visual appeal.

Adding Lush Fillers

Hollow out at least one large head of cabbage to fill with dip.

Fill out the arrangement with large, uncut vegetables that will not be eaten. Wipe off the vegetables, but do not rinse them; produce will stay fresh longer if it has not been washed. Group vegetables together by color, ensuring that color is evenly spaced around the table. Leftover vegetables need not be wasted; use for soups, sautés, or salads.

Place whole vegetables in and around the baskets to build up the foundation.

Fill in with kale leaves.

To make it easy for guests to serve themselves, leave space for plates and napkins.

An Uncommon Blend
At Common Folk Company

At her shop in Centralia, Washington, Ilona Steelhammer combines art, crafts, and cappuccino to create an irresistible treat for Christmas shoppers.

Each holiday season, patrons from near and far head to Common Folk Company, a charming shop located a stone's throw from Interstate 5 about halfway between Seattle and Portland.

Ilona, the owner of Common Folk Company and a popular Northwest artist, fills her comfortable, unpretentious store with an eclectic array of her own oil paintings and crafts, pieces by other folk artists, antiques, and reproduction country furniture.

There's even a coffee bar—with its heavenly

aromas of fresh pastries and steaming cappuccino—to tempt shoppers to linger a bit longer.

The homelike atmosphere is no accident. When Ilona and her husband, Norm, opened Common Folk Company, they intended to use it primarily as a retail outlet for Ilona's oil paintings and limited-edition prints. "I knew I couldn't work and show my paintings out of my home any longer," explains Ilona, "but I didn't want to open a typical art gallery either. I wanted a place where people would feel as

This page and opposite page: Ilona is known for her endearing characters and winning use of color. Old Saint Nick, shown with Ilona in her shop (opposite page), is her latest painting; Snowboy *(above) and* Starry, Starry Night *(right) were painted earlier and have appeared in prints and on Christmas cards.*

comfortable as they did in my home."

So Norm drew up the plans and built an airy, two-story structure—the shop on the first floor, the gallery and Ilona's studio on the second. But Ilona promptly ignored that store/studio distinction and began displaying her paintings as she had in her home. She surrounded each one with country collectibles and folk art pieces that more often than not related thematically to the artwork.

A self-taught artist, Ilona calls the whimsical people in her artwork "common folk" (hence the name of her store). Their homespun pursuits celebrate the simple pleasures of rural life in the Northwest.

Her Christmas paintings also reflect these roots. *Snowboy* was inspired by actual snowmen that popped up all over Centralia after a good snow several years ago. In *Starry, Starry Night*, the animals gathered around the Christ Child—ducks, geese, chickens, sheep, and a cow—might be found in any Washington farmyard.

Sharp-eyed customers may notice a family resemblance between the people in Ilona's paintings and

some of the shop's stuffed dolls and soft-sculpture Santas. Ilona often trades her paintbrush for a needle and makes her common folk in three dimensions.

Ilona crafts about 30 Santas each year, and she searches year-round for the old, well-loved materials that give each one its unique character. "It's almost like a scavenger hunt. I comb secondhand stores for old wool blankets and clothing, and I look through antiques shops for trinkets and miniatures."

For each Santa a body is sewn from woolens, a face is crafted from papier-mâché, and a beard is fashioned from sheep's wool. Then Ilona dresses the figure in handmade clothes and accessories gleaned from her collecting forays.

Ilona's shop is also filled with the creations of other crafters from around the country. "At first I tried to concentrate on the works of Northwest artists," says Ilona, "but I found I couldn't resist what people from other regions were doing."

Her smorgasbord of Santas is a good example. Cheek by jowl with Santas made by a Toledo, Washington, woodcarver are gourd Santas painted by a crafter in Ohio.

Ilona's shop has been a wonderful success, and so far each Christmas has been better than the last. "I opened Common Folk Company in the hopes that it would allow me to be more organized, but if anything my life is crazier than ever before," laughs Ilona. "But when people tell me how much they like the shop, and when I think about how it enables me and other artists to make a living at our craft, then I realize it's all been worth it."

Opposite page: Ilona likes to mix her own handcrafts with those of other artists. She painted the old cupboard and made the chalkware Santas inside it (top left) from a chocolate mold her mother bought in Germany; Ilona also crafted the gold stars that march across the lid of an antique trunk (bottom left). For source listings for the stars, the chalkware, wood, and gourd Santas, and Ilona's prints and cards, see page 153.

Right: Ilona's artwork has appeared in four children's books authored by Stephen Cosgrove, and a series of cards, posters, and prints. For her, creating one-of-a-kind Santas in papier-mâché and fabric is a delightful change of pace.

Bulbs for Winter Blooms

Forcing bulbs is an old holiday custom, and it's easy to understand why: Few sights are more heartening on a bleak winter's day than vivid green leaves topped with cheerful blooms. Brighten your home this season with several containers of forced bulbs, and remember friends with ready-to-grow gifts of bulbs and all the accessories.

Above: Amaryllis look especially festive in pots decorated with your handwritten holiday greetings. Paint the pots with three coats of black chalkboard slating (available at craft and hardware stores) and then write on them with colored chalk.

The bulbs featured here are easy to force, and our source listings on page 153 make them easy to find. (During fall and winter, many nurseries and garden centers also carry bulbs for forcing.)

In our experiments we had great success—every bulb bloomed. But we found that blooming times can vary widely. If you want to have blossoms for a special occasion, start plenty of bulbs over the course of a fortnight or so.

Buy bulbs that are precooled, or pretreated, and ready for forcing. Amaryllis and paperwhite narcissus are almost always sold pretreated; hyacinths often are. To be sure, ask before you buy. If you buy bulbs that are not pretreated, you'll need to cool them for several months in a refrigerator or unheated garage, porch, or basement.

The blooming times mentioned below are for pretreated bulbs and refer to the time period after the bulbs are brought into the sun.

Amaryllis

Using a good potting soil, plant the bulb in a six- or eight-inch clay pot so that the top half of the bulb is exposed. Water thoroughly and then keep the soil fairly dry until top growth starts; afterward, water when the soil feels dry to the touch. Move the pot to a warm, sunny spot. You may need to insert a stake alongside the bulb to support the stalk as it develops.

Blooming Time: two to eight weeks.

Paperwhite Narcissus

You may grow narcissus in potting soil or in pebbles.

If using potting soil, select a container that is at least twice as tall as the bulbs. Plant the bulbs one-half inch apart and with their tops exposed. Water whenever the soil feels dry to the touch.

If using pebbles, select a shallow container and fill it with pebbles. (The saucers from large clay pots are inexpensive and work well. However, be sure to line them with plastic saucers, since the clay weeps and the moisture can damage tabletops.) Half-bury the bulbs in the pebbles and maintain a layer of water just below the bottom of the bulbs.

Place the container in a cool, dark location. When the bulbs have developed roots and leaves, move them to a warm, sunny spot.

Blooming Time: three to six weeks.

Hyacinth

You may grow hyacinths in potting soil or in special containers called hyacinth vases or hyacinth glasses. If using potting soil, follow the directions for planting paperwhite narcissus.

If using hyacinth vases, merely fill each vase with water and set a bulb into the opening. Maintain a water level just below the bottom of the bulb.

Place containers in a cool, dark location. When the bulbs have developed roots and leaves, move them to a warm, sunny spot.

Blooming Time: three to six weeks.

Above: As festive as poinsettias, fragrant paperwhite narcissus herald the season. Wrap up everything a friend will need to grow of her own: a container filled with bags of bulbs and pebbles and a card with instructions for forcing. We used paper lunch sacks and a plain card; to jazz them up, we burnished the sacks and feathered the edges of the card with copper Rub 'n Buff and tied the sacks with garnet ribbons.

Left: Snowy white hyacinths in full bloom smell as sweet as they look. Hyacinth vases were all the rage during the Victorian and Edwardian periods, and these days they're making a comeback. Because antique hyacinth vases are highly collectible, both replicas and new vases are popping up in gardening catalogs. For source listings for antique and new vases, see page 153.

Patterns

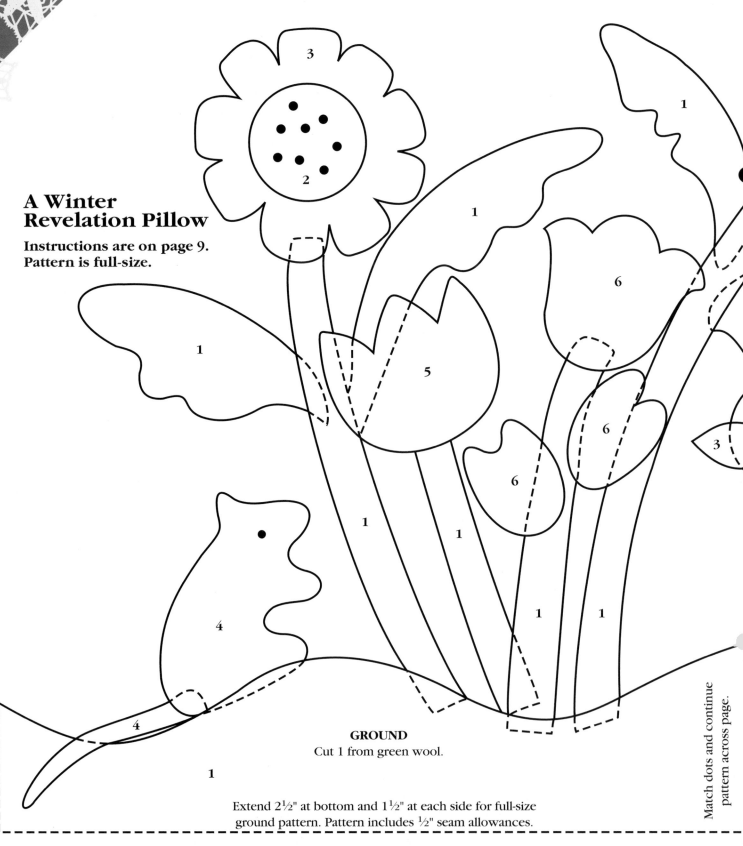

A Winter Revelation Pillow

Instructions are on page 9.
Pattern is full-size.

GROUND
Cut 1 from green wool.

Extend 2½" at bottom and 1½" at each side for full-size ground pattern. Pattern includes ½" seam allowances.

Match dots and continue pattern across page.

3

3

3

1

1

1

2

2

2

3

3

1

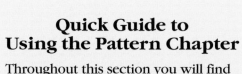

Quick Guide to Using the Pattern Chapter

Throughout this section you will find guidelines and handy tips for using the patterns. In addition, where possible, we have suggested other uses for the patterns so that you can create different looks or additional projects.

Look for boxes on enlarging and transferring the patterns and on how to tailor the projects to your own needs.

Here is a list of helpful tools you may want to have on hand when drafting and transferring patterns: tracing paper, carbon paper, dressmaker's carbon paper, a dressmaker's pen, a water-soluble marker, a black felt-tipped permanent marker, a pencil, white and colored pencils, and a ruler.

129

Canvas Snowman

Instructions are on page 14.
Patterns are full-size and include ¼"
seam allowances.

HAT CROWN
Cut 2 from black felt.

Leave open.

Extend body 2" at bottom. Leave open.

BODY
Cut 2 from white canvas.

Match dots and
continue pattern across page.

Place on fold.

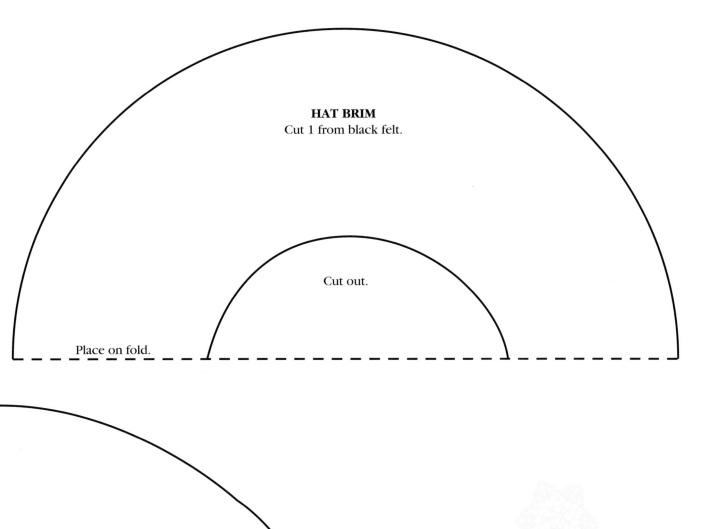

HAT BRIM
Cut 1 from black felt.

Cut out.

Place on fold.

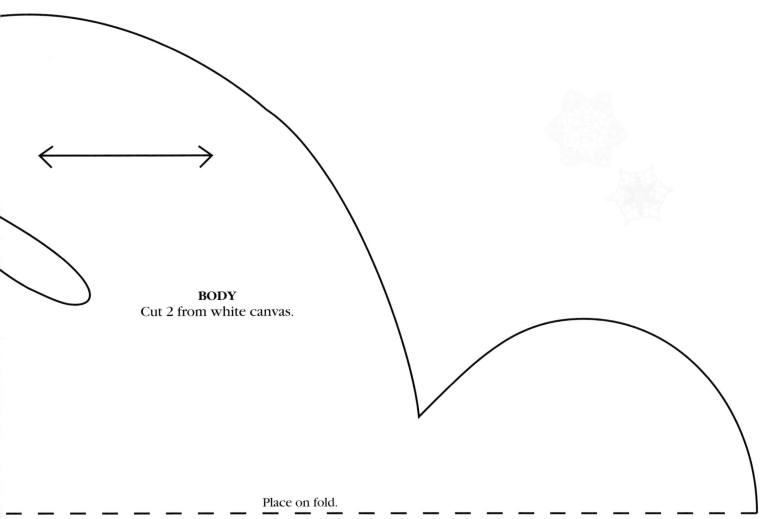

BODY
Cut 2 from white canvas.

Place on fold.

Very Merry Santaberries

**Instructions begin on page 29.
Patterns are full-size.**

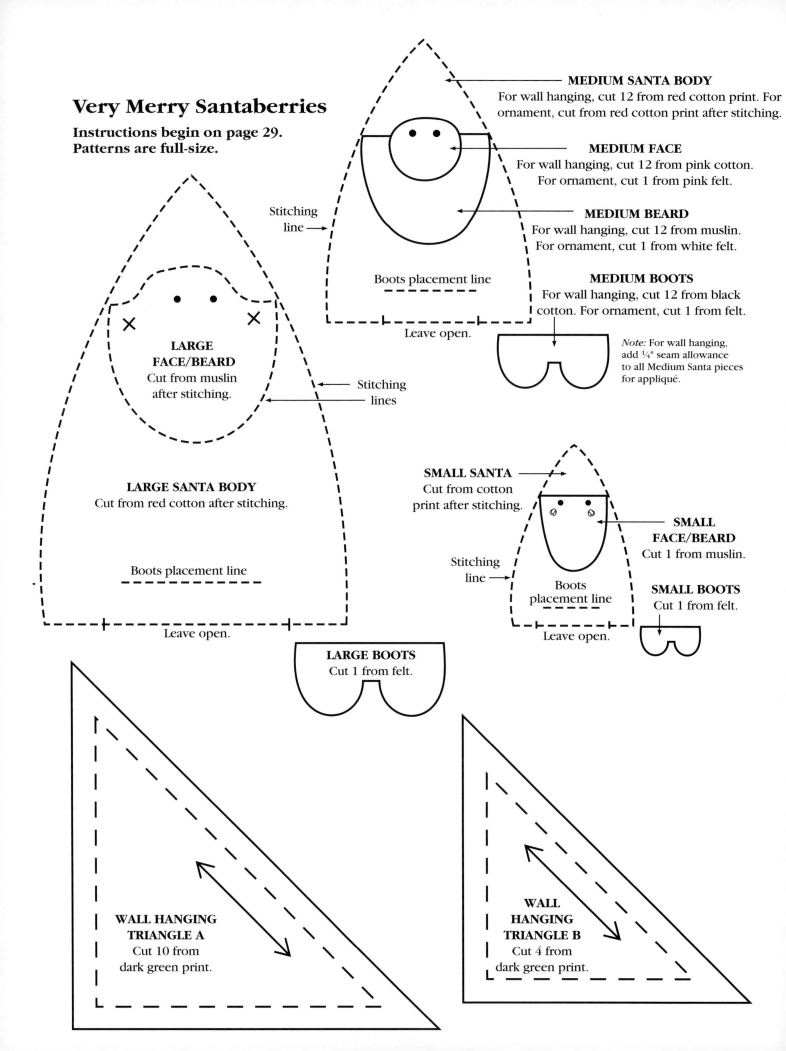

MEDIUM SANTA BODY

For wall hanging, cut 12 from red cotton print. For ornament, cut from red cotton print after stitching.

MEDIUM FACE

For wall hanging, cut 12 from pink cotton. For ornament, cut 1 from pink felt.

MEDIUM BEARD

For wall hanging, cut 12 from muslin. For ornament, cut 1 from white felt.

MEDIUM BOOTS

For wall hanging, cut 12 from black cotton. For ornament, cut 1 from felt.

Note: For wall hanging, add ¼" seam allowance to all Medium Santa pieces for appliqué.

Stitching line →

Boots placement line

Leave open.

**LARGE
FACE/BEARD**
Cut from muslin
after stitching.

← Stitching
lines

LARGE SANTA BODY
Cut from red cotton after stitching.

Boots placement line

Leave open.

SMALL SANTA
Cut from cotton
print after stitching.

**SMALL
FACE/BEARD**
Cut 1 from muslin.

Stitching
line →

Boots
placement line

SMALL BOOTS
Cut 1 from felt.

Leave open.

LARGE BOOTS
Cut 1 from felt.

**WALL HANGING
TRIANGLE A**
Cut 10 from
dark green print.

**WALL
HANGING
TRIANGLE B**
Cut 4 from
dark green print.

On, Dasher!

Instructions are on page 33.

Color Key

Symbol	DMC	Color
-		White
■	310	Black
♥	315	Antique Mauve-vy. dk.
r	316	Antique Mauve-med.
=	352	Coral-lt.
:	353	Peach
+	414	Steel Gray-dk.
e	611	Drab Brown-dk.
●	796	Royal Blue-dk.
❖	991	Aquamarine-dk.
u	993	Aquamarine-lt.
☆	3046	Yellow Beige-med.
✛	3687	Mauve

Note: Numbers are for DMC floss. Cross-stitch over 1 thread, using 3 strands of floss. Use 1 strand of 310 Black for backstitching and for French knots for children's eyes.

Woolly Stocking

Instructions are on page 35.

Each square equals 1".

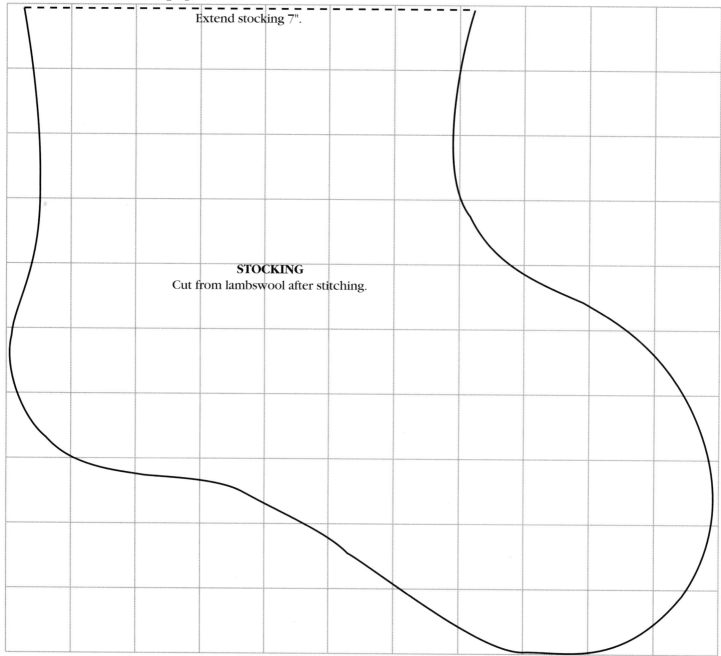

Extend stocking 7".

STOCKING
Cut from lambswool after stitching.

Enlarging Patterns

There are two commonly used ways to enlarge patterns—drawing a grid and using a copy machine. To use the grid method, you will need plain, graph, or butcher paper. Tape pieces together for large patterns. Use a colored pencil and a ruler to draw a 1" grid or the size indicated on the pattern. Using a different colored pencil, copy the original pattern square by square onto the enlarged grid. (Visually divide each grid line into fourths to determine the exact point that the pattern line intersects the grid line.)

To use a copy machine, enlarge the pattern on the copy machine until each square of the grid measures 1" or the required size.

You should note whether seam allowances are included in the pattern or if they need to be added after the pattern is enlarged.

Woolly Birds

Instructions are on page 35.
Patterns are full-size.

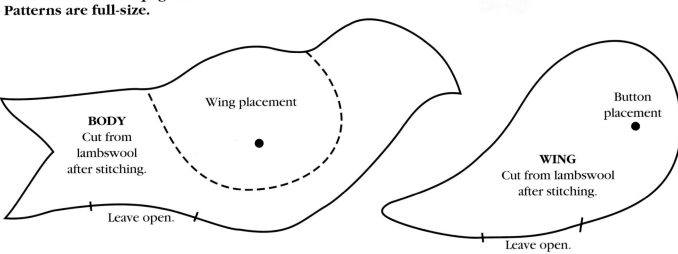

BODY
Cut from lambswool after stitching.

Wing placement

Leave open.

WING
Cut from lambswool after stitching.

Button placement

Leave open.

Paper Heart Garlands

Instructions are on page 36.
Patterns are full-size.

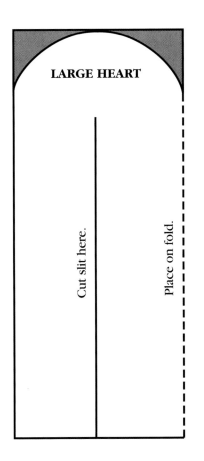

LARGE HEART

Cut slit here.

Place on fold.

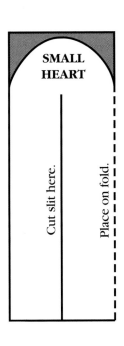

SMALL HEART

Cut slit here.

Place on fold.

This sophisticated all-white garland can also be made out of brightly colored construction paper for a childlike look. In addition to the garland, make individual hearts to use as ornaments or package toppers.

135

Trio of Angels

Instructions are on page 37.
Patterns are full-size.

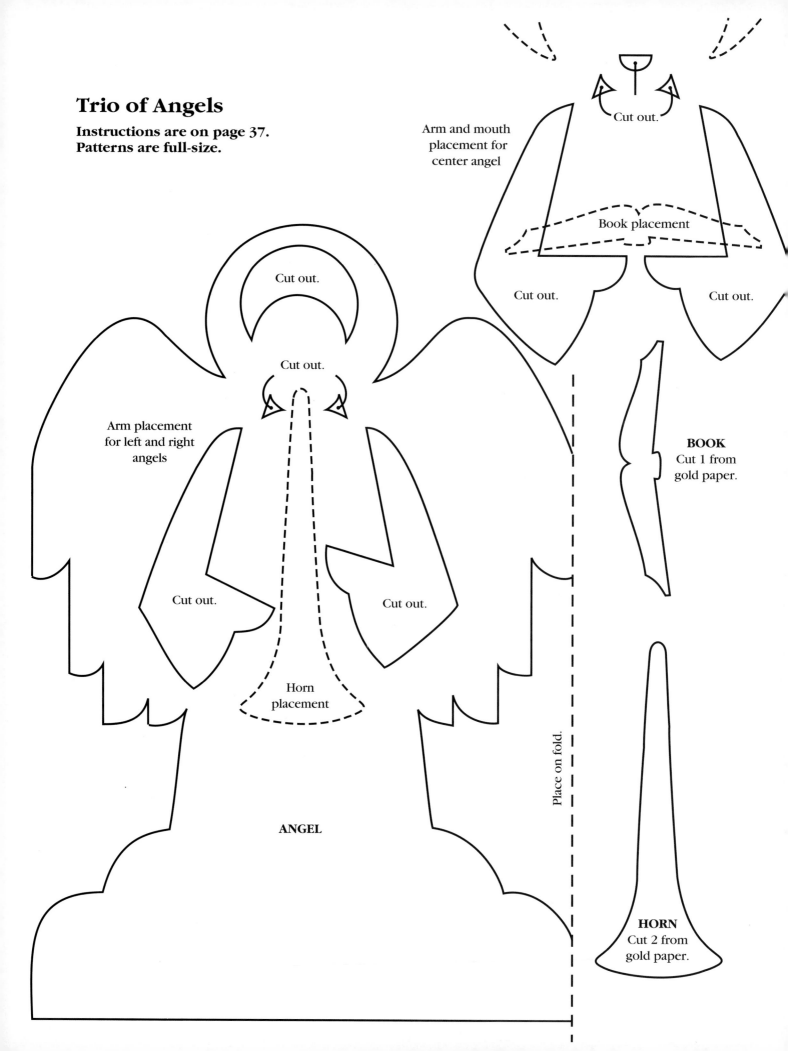

Arm and mouth placement for center angel

Cut out.

Book placement

Cut out.

Cut out.

Cut out.

Cut out.

Arm placement for left and right angels

Cut out.

Cut out.

Horn placement

ANGEL

Place on fold.

BOOK
Cut 1 from gold paper.

HORN
Cut 2 from gold paper.

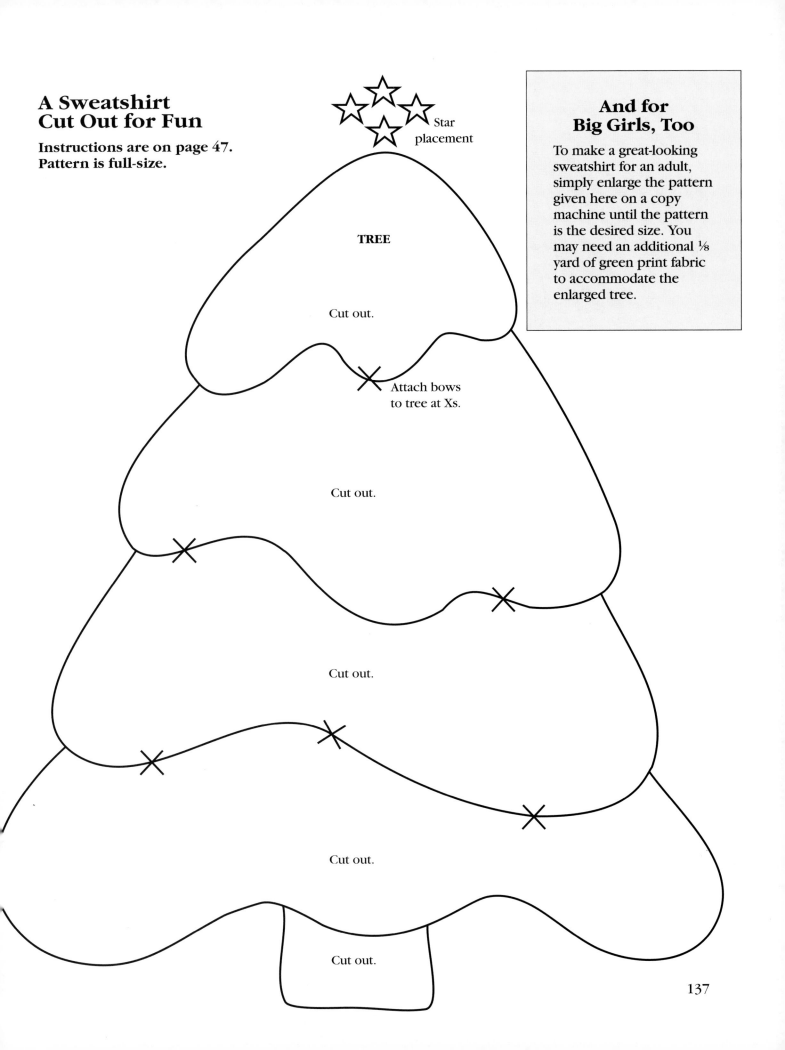

A Sweatshirt
Cut Out for Fun

**Instructions are on page 47.
Pattern is full-size.**

Star
placement

TREE

Cut out.

✗ Attach bows
to tree at Xs.

Cut out.

✗

✗

Cut out.

✗

✗

Cut out.

✗

Cut out.

Cut out.

And for
Big Girls, Too

To make a great-looking
sweatshirt for an adult,
simply enlarge the pattern
given here on a copy
machine until the pattern
is the desired size. You
may need an additional ⅛
yard of green print fabric
to accommodate the
enlarged tree.

137

Fashion a Fine Humpty Dumpty

Instructions are on page 32.
Patterns are full-size and include ¼" seam allowances.

FACIAL FEATURES

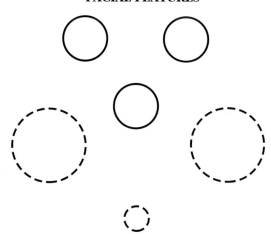

Attach snaps for eyes and button for nose. Straightstitch outline of cheeks and mouth red. Fill in cheeks with blush.

HEAD
Cut 2 from quilted muslin.
Reverse and cut 2 more.

Center seam

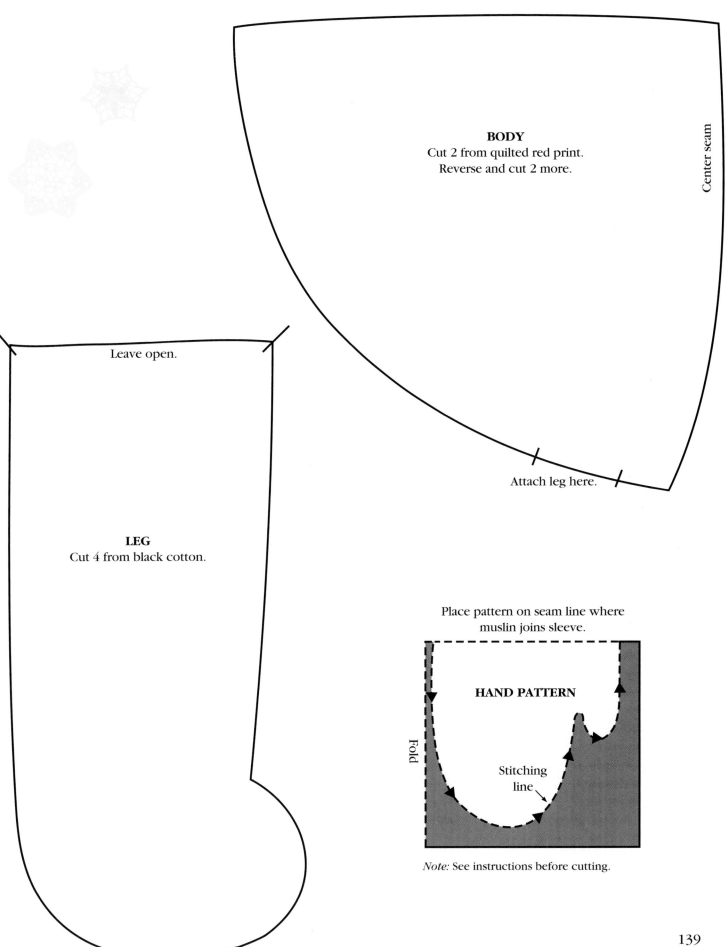

BODY
Cut 2 from quilted red print.
Reverse and cut 2 more.

Center seam

Leave open.

Attach leg here.

LEG
Cut 4 from black cotton.

Place pattern on seam line where
muslin joins sleeve.

HAND PATTERN

Fold

Stitching
line

Note: See instructions before cutting.

139

Christmas Tree Sprites

Instructions are on page 49.
Pattern is full-size.

These ethereal ornaments make great gifts for many special occasions. Give a bright-eyed nymph to a friend for her birthday, or to anyone who might need a little fairy to bring her smiles throughout the year.

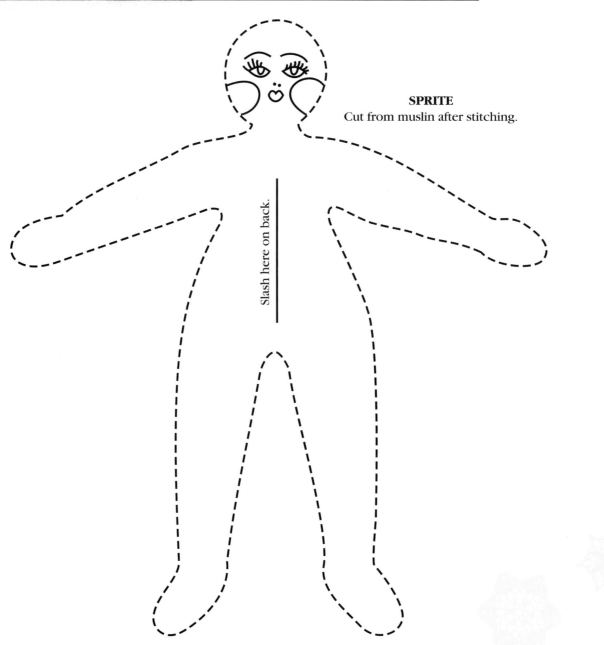

SPRITE
Cut from muslin after stitching.

Slash here on back.

140

Jewelry in Gingerbread and Spongeware

Instructions begin on page 52.
Patterns are full-size.

Gingerbread Pins

Place heart here.

STAR
Cut 1.

Place star here.

TREE
Cut 1.

Place heart here.

ANGEL
Cut 1.

Place heart here.

MAN
Cut 1.

Place heart here.

HEART
Cut 1.

Transferring Patterns

The method you use for transferring the pattern will depend on the type of material to which the pattern is being transferred.

For simple patterns that are to be transferred to most any fabric, the easiest method is to lay the tracing paper on the pattern; then trace and cut out around the outline. Pin the pattern to the fabric and trace around the pattern. In addition, there are variations to this method:

For light-colored, lightweight fabric or paper, trace or copy the pattern. Retrace the outline with a black marker. Tape the tracing to a window pane or light box; then tape the material over the tracing. Using a water-soluble marker, trace the pattern onto the material.

For solid or opaque materials such as dark fabric, card-stock paper, wood, or plastic, trace the pattern. Stack the material (right side up), the carbon paper (carbon side down), and the tracing of the pattern (right side up). With a dull pencil, trace over the pattern to transfer the carbon outline to the material.

For materials such as dough, modeling compounds, or clay, trace and cut out the pattern. Place the pattern on the material and, using a knife or pointed object, mark outline on the material. Cut out along the outline.

When one-half of the pattern is given (as indicated by a dashed line on the pattern), fold the tracing paper in half and place the fold on the dashed line of the pattern. Trace the pattern half and cut out through both layers. Unfold for the full pattern.

When transferring patterns, always transfer all placement and guide markings as well as the outline to the tracing paper.

Jewelry patterns continued on next page.

Spongeware Jewelry

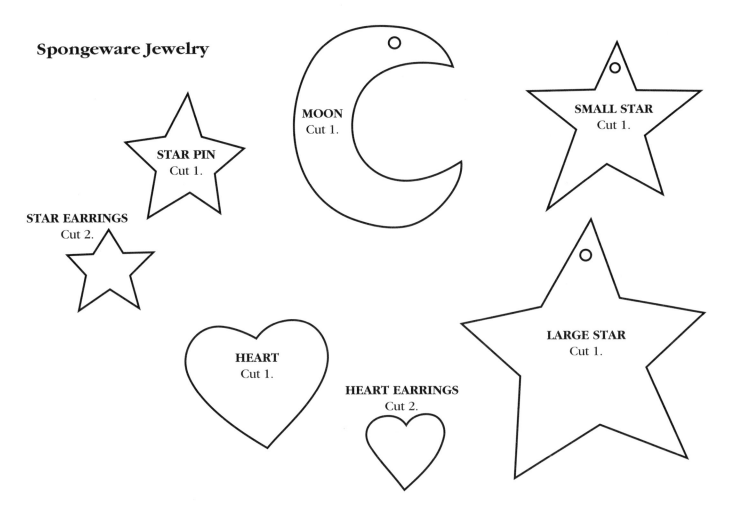

MOON
Cut 1.

SMALL STAR
Cut 1.

STAR PIN
Cut 1.

STAR EARRINGS
Cut 2.

LARGE STAR
Cut 1.

HEART
Cut 1.

HEART EARRINGS
Cut 2.

Strawberry Clusters

**Instructions are on page 63.
Patterns are full-size.**

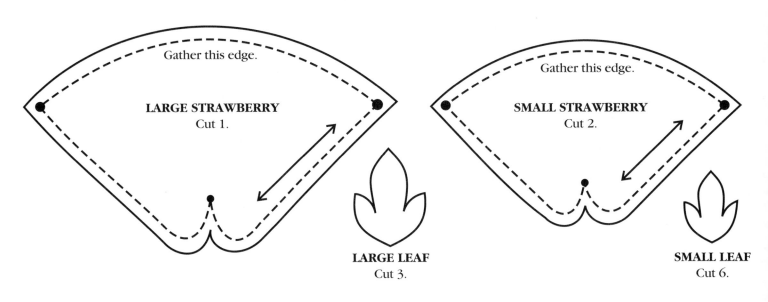

Gather this edge.

LARGE STRAWBERRY
Cut 1.

Gather this edge.

SMALL STRAWBERRY
Cut 2.

LARGE LEAF
Cut 3.

SMALL LEAF
Cut 6.

Woolen Santa Ornament

Instructions are on page 70.
Patterns are full-size and include ¼" seam allowances, unless otherwise noted.

Embroidery Placement Diagram

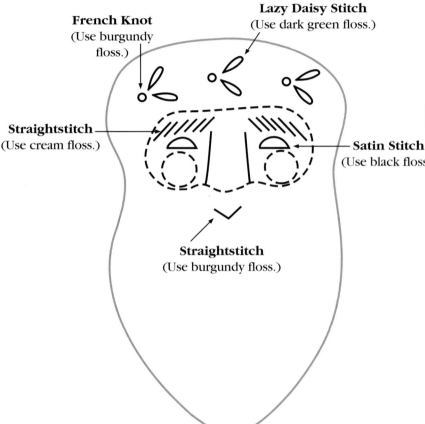

French Knot
(Use burgundy floss.)

Lazy Daisy Stitch
(Use dark green floss.)

Straightstitch
(Use cream floss.)

Satin Stitch
(Use black floss.)

Straightstitch
(Use burgundy floss.)

HAT
Cut 2 from burgundy wool.

For face, cut out ⅛" within dotted line in front piece only. See instructions before cutting.

HEAD
Cut 2 from cream wool.

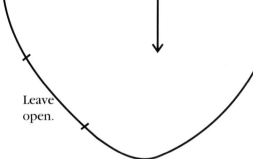

Leave open.

Embroidery Tips

Different types of embroidery require different types of needles. For working on tightly woven fabrics such as wool or cotton, use a needle that has a sharp point, such as an embroidery or chenille needle. For cross-stitch, needlepoint, or other counted-thread embroidery, use a tapestry needle, which has a blunt point.

Work with yarns or threads cut no longer than 18 inches; an extremely long thread, pulled too often through the fabric, tends to knot and fray.

Whenever possible, use a frame or hoop. It keeps the fabric flat and smooth and the stitches even.

Victorian Cut-Paper Ornaments

**Instructions are on page 62.
Patterns are full-size.**

Place lace trim here.

FLOWER SHOE
Cut 1 from cardboard and
1 from black paper.

Place lace trim here.

Victorian Variations

In addition to the trims mentioned in the note on page 62, you can also adorn your Victorian ornaments with glitter, miniature ribbon flowers or bows, or rickrack.

Other traditional Victorian shapes include vases, dolls, hot-air balloons, animals, anchors, and crosses. Look for "scrap" pictures of children, fruit, or fashion ladies to decorate the ornaments.

Place lace trim here.

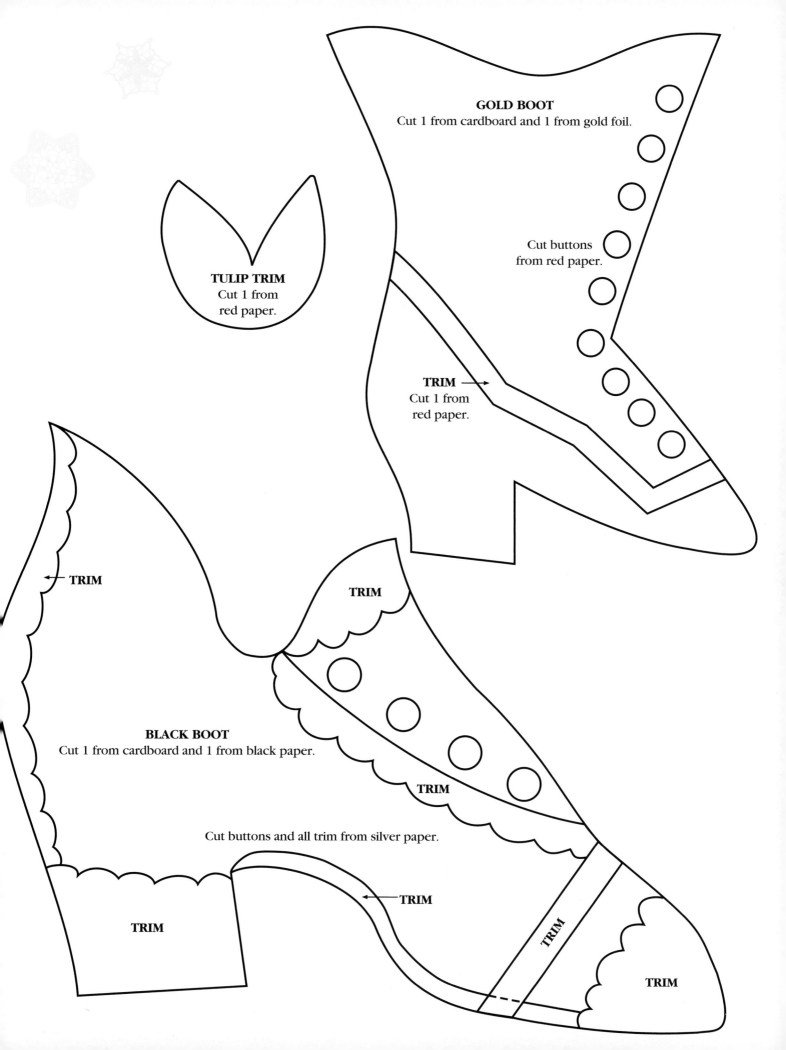

GOLD BOOT
Cut 1 from cardboard and 1 from gold foil.

Cut buttons
from red paper.

TULIP TRIM
Cut 1 from
red paper.

TRIM
Cut 1 from
red paper.

TRIM

TRIM

TRIM

BLACK BOOT
Cut 1 from cardboard and 1 from black paper.

TRIM

Cut buttons and all trim from silver paper.

TRIM

TRIM

TRIM

TRIM

Snowflake Cookies

**Instructions are on page 87.
Pattern is full-size.**

Spool Shelf

**Instructions are on page 38.
Patterns are full-size.**

TOP OF BACK PIECE
Position pattern ¼" from top end of pine.

Since each of these cookies is a work of art in itself, a snowflake makes a delectable gift. Wrap individual cookies in clear cellophane and tie with sparkling white ribbon to give to friends at work or in the neighborhood. These glimmering cookies are also an elegant dessert for an intimate winter wedding or shower.

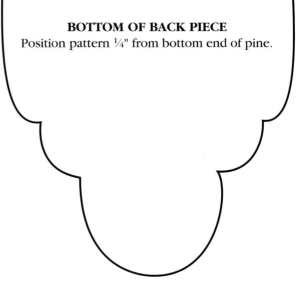

BOTTOM OF BACK PIECE
Position pattern ¼" from bottom end of pine.

146

Squirrel and Acorn Chart

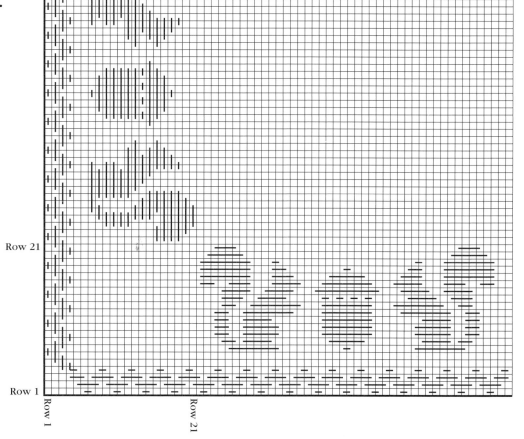

Darn These Napkins

Instructions are on page 83.

Note: Stitch the napkins with the following pearl cotton colors:

Squirrels and Acorns—rust
Border—dark green

Reindeer—dark brown
Border—maroon

Cows—black
Border—dark green

Row 21

Row 1

Row 1

Row 21

Reindeer Chart

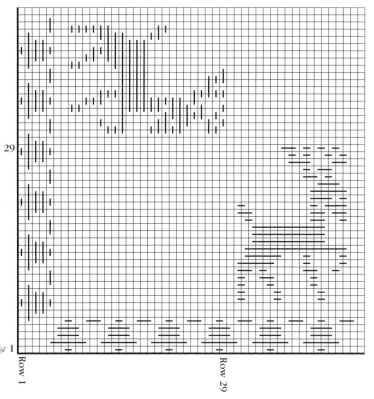

29

1

Row 1

Row 29

Cow Chart

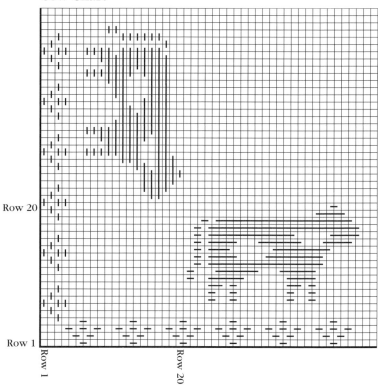

Row 20

Row 1

Row 1

Row 20

147

Stenciled Tablecloth

Instructions begin on page 94.
Patterns are full-size.

Note: Make stencils for ¼ of design, according to pattern. Refer to placement lines to stencil complete design. Broken lines are placement lines.

BLOCK STENCIL: ONE-FOURTH PATTERN

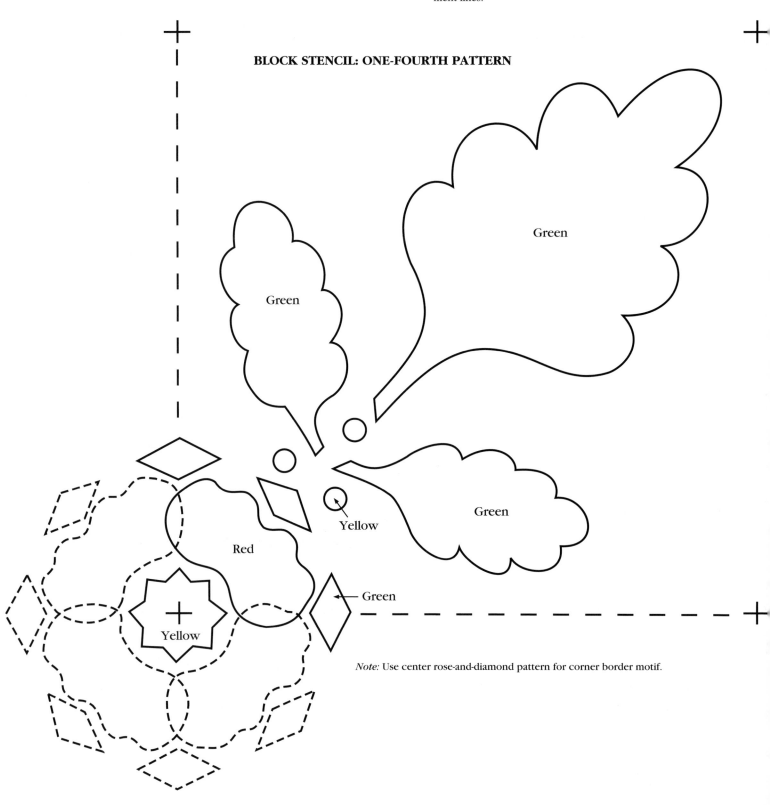

Green

Green

Green

Yellow

Red

Green

Yellow

Note: Use center rose-and-diamond pattern for corner border motif.

BORDER STENCIL

Place on fold line of border strip.

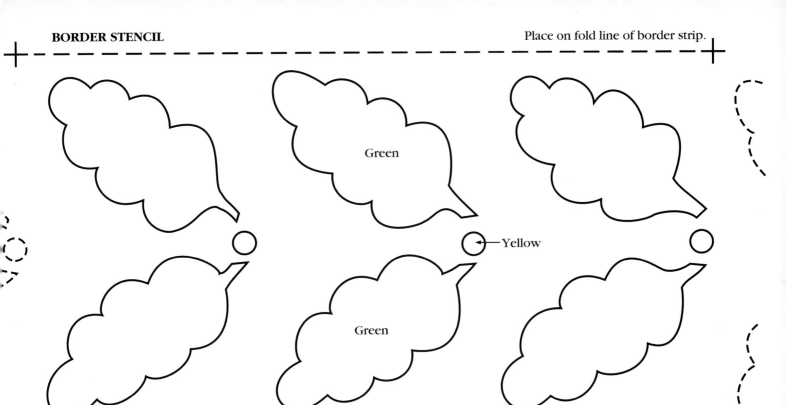

Repeat pattern to complete border.

SASHING STENCIL

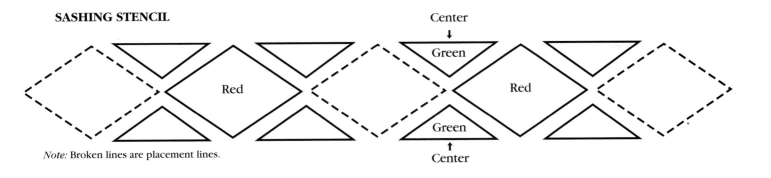

Note: Broken lines are placement lines.

More Stenciling Ideas

The stenciling patterns used in the tablecloth lend themselves to a number of applications. You can make matching napkins in a variety of ways: For each napkin, stencil the rose-and-diamond motif only in the corner; then edge the napkin with a colorful binding as shown here. Or trim the edges of a napkin with the sashing motif or stencil the entire block motif on the napkins.

The block motif would also make a gorgeous holiday pillow to decorate a sofa or bed. Stencil the border motif on the pillow flange or ruffle. Use the tablecloth as a dynamic wall hanging by adding hanging tabs to the back of the finished piece.

A Card Full of Wishful Whiskers

Patterns are full-size.
Instructions are on page 113.

BOW

Cut 1 from red paper.
Reverse and cut 1 more.

STAR
Cut 2 from yellow paper.

CAT
Cut 1 from
black paper.

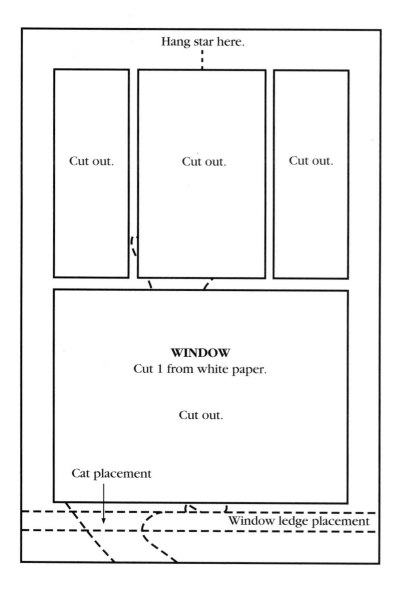

Hang star here.

Cut out.

Cut out.

Cut out.

WINDOW
Cut 1 from white paper.

Cut out.

Cat placement

Window ledge placement

WINDOW LEDGE
Cut 1 from white paper.

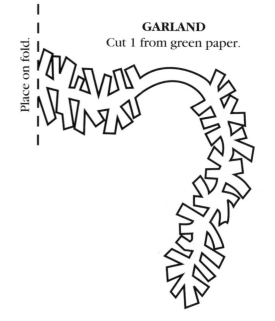

Place on fold.

GARLAND
Cut 1 from green paper.

A Feast-Your-Eyes Tablescape

Instructions are on page 121.

This shopping list is a guide for purchasing the produce. It includes vegetables that are used both for building the base and for eating. Make substitutions as desired.

Market Order

3 heads green cabbage with large outer leaves
2 heads red cabbage
4 heads cauliflower
1 head broccoflower
2 bunches broccoli
6 to 8 bunches kale
10 sweet red bell peppers
5 green bell peppers
1 pound large mushrooms
1 bunch green beans
1 bunch carrots with tops
1 large bunch carrots, cleaned
5 winter squash

Crocheted Snowflakes

Instructions begin on page 59.

Crochet Abbreviations

beg—beginning	**sc**—single crochet
ch—chain(s)	**sk**—skip
dc—double crochet	**sl st**—slip stitch
dec—decrease	**sp(s)**—space(s)
lp(s)—loop(s)	**st(s)**—stitch(es)
rep—repeat	**tr**—triple crochet
rnd(s)—round(s)	**yo**—yarn over

Candles Dressed in Silver and Gold

Instructions are on page 20.

The Bay Essentials

The bay leaf, a member of the laurel family, is the symbol of dignity, victory, and glory. Glorify your own projects by adding it to your list of craft materials. Bay can be quite expensive for craft use, especially if you buy the small spice containers of leaves from your local grocery store. Many health and organic food stores sell herbs and spices in bulk, and bay leaves can be purchased less expensively in this way. In addition, you can order them through herbal companies, which is often the surest way to get large, whole, uncrushed leaves. For information on ordering bay leaves, see the source listing on page 153.

Sources

◆ Cover—beeswax tapers: The Museum Store at the Heritage Center of Lancaster County, 13 West King Street, Lancaster, PA 17603, or call 717-393-3364.

◆ Cover—candle clips: for catalog send $3.00 to D. Blümchen & Company, Inc., P.O. Box 1210, Ridgewood, NJ 07451-1210, or call 201-652-5595.

◆ Cover—fresh greenery delivered to your door: Laurel Springs Fraser Firs, P.O. Box 85, Laurel Springs, NC 28644, or call 800-851-2345.

◆ Page 4—red cabinet: Butch Robins, P.O. Box 455, Seabrook, TX 77586, or call 713-474-7387.

◆ Page 5—hand-carved crafts: P. J. Hornberger Gallery, P.O. Box 4, New Ulm, TX 78950, or call 409-992-3900.

◆ Page 6—dried materials and finished wreaths:

Texas General Store, 2200–A Bayport Blvd., Seabrook, TX 77586, or call 800-982-9828.

◆ Page 16—Frank Lloyd Wright Home and Studio Gift Catalog: 411 Harrison Street, Oak Park, IL 60304-1427, or call 708-848-9518.

◆ Page 20—dried bay leaves: Texas General Store, 2200–A Bayport Blvd., Seabrook, TX 77586, or call 800-982-9828.

◆ Page 24—Mailbox Huggie Frame: Best Buy Floral Supply, P.O. Box 1982, Cedar Rapids, IA 52406, or call 800-553-8497, or 800-332-5299 in Iowa.

◆ Page 35—buttons: Buttons and Things, 24 Main Street, Freeport, ME 04032, or call 207-865-4480.

buttons: for catalog send $1.00 to Clotilde, Inc., P.O. Box 22312, Dept. OH, Fort Lauderdale, FL 33315-2312, or call 305-761-8655.

◆ Page 40—vinegar-grained creations: for brochure send $1.00 and SASE to Fanciful Graining, 706 Brownsville Road, Sinking Spring, PA 19608.

◆ Page 42—unfinished handmade frames: Eisenhower's Wood Works, 80 Lake Road, Fleetwood, PA 19522.

◆ Page 50—buttons: Buttons and Things, 24 Main Street, Freeport, ME 04032, or call 207-865-4480.

buttons: for catalog send $1.00 to Clotilde, Inc., P.O. Box 22312, Dept. OH, Fort Lauderdale, FL 33315-2312, or call 305-761-8655.

vintage buttons: Tender Buttons, 143 East 62nd Street, New York, NY 10021, or call 212-758-7004.

vintage buttons: Tender Buttons, 946 North Rush Street, Chicago, IL 60611, or call 312-337-7033.

◆ Page 62—scrap pictures: Gerlachs of Lecha, P.O. Box 213, Emmaus, PA 18049, or call 215-965-9181.

scrap pictures: for catalog send $3.00 to D. Blümchen & Company, Inc., P.O. Box 1210, Ridgewood, NJ 07451-1210, or call 201-652-5595.

◆ Page 65—steamed pudding mold: Williams-Sonoma, Mail Order Dept.,

P.O. Box 7456, San Francisco, CA 94120-7456, or call 800-541-2233.

◆ Page 67—tiny aspic cutters: for catalog send $2.00 to Maid of Scandinavia, 3244 Raleigh Ave., Minneapolis, MN 55416, or call 800-328-6722.

◆ Page 69—Christopher Radko ornaments: for color catalog send $7.50 to Christmas at the Zoo, 118 Northwest 23rd Ave., Portland, OR 97210, or call 503-223-4048.

Christopher Radko ornaments: for color catalog send $7.00 to M. Collectables DBA, The Christmas Shop, 18 Bishop Ct., Savannah, GA 31401, or call 912-234-5343.

Christopher Radko ornaments: for color catalog send $6.00 to Margo's Gift Shop, 2058 Yorktown Alley, Utica Square, Tulsa, OK 74114, or call 918-747-8780.

Christopher Radko ornaments: Vinny's Showplace, 1076 South Colony Rd., Wallingford, CT 06492, or call 203-265-9309.

◆ Page 69—*Starlight* newsletter: to receive quarterly newsletter and voucher for a collectible ornament send $15.00 to Starlight Family of Collectors, Planetarium Station, P.O. Box 770, New York, NY 10024-05393, or call 212-362-5344.

◆ Page 69—tree stand: Pacific Christmas Trees, 23855 SW 195th Place, Sherwood, OR 97140, or call 503-625-7966.

◆ Pages 77, 79—Christmas tree pasta: Buckeye Beans & Herbs, P.O. Box 28201, Spokane, WA 99228-8201, or call 509-926-9963.

◆ Page 82—sealing wax and stamp "metal ring": Victorian Papers, P.O. Box 411341, Kansas City, MO 64141-1341, or call 800-800-6647.

◆ Page 83—Heritage napkins: Wichelt Imports, Inc., Route 1, Box 139, Stoddard, WI 54658.

◆ Page 86—tiny aspic cutters: for catalog send $2.00 to Maid of Scandinavia, 3244 Raleigh Ave., Minneapolis, MN 55416, or call 800-328-6722.

◆ Page 87—edible glitter: for catalog send $2.00 to Maid of Scandinavia, 3244 Raleigh Ave., Minneapolis, MN 55416, or call 800-328-6722.

◆ Page 108—duplicate-stitch graphing system: for catalog send $1.00 and SASE to Nancy Claytor Designs, 217 East Liberty Street, York, SC 29745, or call 803-684-6815.

◆ Page 108—cross-stitch graphing system: for catalog send $1.00 and SASE to Nancy Claytor Designs, 217 East Liberty Street, York, SC 29745, or call 803-684-6815.

◆ Page 109—Make-A-Plate: Makit Products, Inc., P.O. Box 769003, Dallas, TX 75376-9003, or call 214-330-7774.

◆ Page 117—Christmas cracker kits: for catalog send $3.00 to D. Blümchen & Company, Inc., P.O. Box 1210, Ridgewood, NJ 07451-1210, or call 201-652-5595.

Christmas cracker kits: Gerlachs of Lecha, P.O. Box 213, Emmaus, PA 18049, or call 215-965-9181.

Christmas crackers: Lands' End, 1 Lands' End Lane, Dodgeville, WI 53595, or call 800-356-4444.

Christmas crackers: The Horchow Collection, P.O. Box 620048, Dallas, TX 75262-0048, or call 800-456-7000.

◆ Page 120—catering services: Kathy G's Catering, Inc., 300 22nd Avenue South, Birmingham, AL 35205.

◆ Page 125—gold stars, chalkware Santas, artwork, and cards: Common Folk Co., 125 East High Street, Centralia, WA 98531, or call 206-736-8066.

◆ Page 125—painted gourd Santas: Northern Friends, P.O. Box 17119, Chattanooga, TN 37415, or call 800-272-2474.

◆ Page 125—wooden Santas: Chestnut Lane Creations Ltd., 1009 Chestnut, Atlantic, IA 50022, or call 712-243-4014.

◆ Page 126—bulbs: White Flower Farm, Route 63, Litchfield, CT 06759, or call 800-944-9624.

bulbs: McClure & Zimmerman, P.O. Box 368, Friesland, WI 53935, or call 414-326-4220.

◆ Page 127—hyacinth vases: Gardeners Eden, P.O. Box 7307, San Francisco, CA 94120-7307, or call 800-822-9600.

antique hyacinth vases: Alan M. Goffman, 264 East 78th Street, New York, NY 10021, or call 212-517-8192.

◆ Page 151—fresh bay leaves: Bay Laurel Farm, West Garzas Road, Carmel Valley, CA 93924, or call 408-659-2913.

Contributors

Special Thanks

◆ Thanks to the following people who have shared their talents:
Rex Bowman
Charlotte I. Hagood
Margaret Allen Northen
Cecilia Robinson
Jennifer E. Todd

◆ Thanks to the following homeowners in Alabama: Mr. and Mrs. Michael H. Blades; Beth Cook; Judy Gilbert; Eric and Diana Hansen; Jo Harris; Mr. and Mrs. J. Brooke Johnston; Barbara Manning; Celia McGarity; Glenda Parker; Kit Samford; Katherine Sims; Mr. and Mrs. W. Stancil Starnes; Gloria Steiner; Barbara Stone; Mr. and Mrs. James A. Todd, Jr.; Dr. and Mrs. James C. Walker, Jr.

◆ Our thanks also to the following shops in Birmingham, Alabama, for sharing their resources: Bromberg's; Frankie Engel Antiques; The Holly Tree; Jack 'n' Jill Shop; Thread Bear; and Vincent's Market.

Index

Recipes